HISTORIC HERALDIC FAMILIES

HISTORIC
HERALDIC FAMILIES

KEITH B. POOLE

Illustrations by
K. B. Steadman

DAVID & CHARLES
NEWTON ABBOT   LONDON   VANCOUVER

ISBN 0 7153 6839 7

Set in 11 on 13pt Garamond and printed in
Great Britain by Latimer Trend & Company Ltd Plymouth
for David & Charles (Holdings) Limited
South Devon House   Newton Abbot   Devon

Published in Canada
by Douglas David & Charles Limited
132 Philip Avenue   North Vancouver   BC

'The wonder is not that these
families existed but that
they survived at all.'

Sir Bernard Burke

To the memory of
my son

CONTENTS

English Families

Name	Area	page
Badlesmere	Kent	9
Berkeley	Gloucestershire	14
Brocas	Hampshire, Surrey	21
Browne, Viscounts Montagu	Sussex	29
Courtenay, Earls of Devon	Devonshire	34
Disney	Essex, Lincolnshire, America	42
Dymoke	Lincolnshire	49
Fettiplace	Oxfordshire, Berkshire, America	56
Fitzwarine	Berkshire, Oxfordshire	66
Grenville, Dukes of Buckingham and Chandos	Buckinghamshire	72
Herbert, Earls of Pembroke and Montgomery	Wiltshire	78
Killigrew	Cornwall	84
Lovel	Oxfordshire	92
Nevill of Raby, Earls of Westmoreland	Co Durham	98
Paulet, Earls Poulett	Somerset, Hampshire	106
Percy, Earls of Northumberland	Northumberland	113

7

Name	*Area*	*page*
Poyntz	Berkshire, Gloucestershire, Sussex, Ireland	120
Turberville	Dorset	125

Scottish Families

Campbell, Dukes of Argyll	Scotland, Commonwealth, America	131
Hamilton, Dukes of Hamilton & Brandon	Leicestershire, Scotland, Commonwealth	138
Macdonald, Barons Macdonald of Macdonald	Yorkshire, Scotland, Canada	145
Maclean of Duart	Scotland, Commonwealth, America	152
Mackenzie, Earls of Seaforth	Scotland, Canada, America	159
Bibliography		166
Acknowledgements		168

BADLESMERE

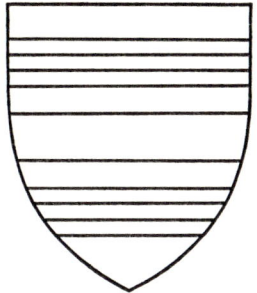

Arms: Argent, a fess between two bars gemelles gules.

Leeds Castle, home of the ill-fated Barons de Badlesmere for a few historic and dramatic years, stands in picturesque splendour some six miles south-east of Maidstone, in Kent, and half a mile south of the London road to Ashford.

This magnificent white stone castle stands in 502 acres of parkland, and in the midst of a lake of some fifteen to twenty acres wide, the waters of which brilliantly reflect it, especially in the summer time when it shines like marble amongst the thousands of floating water lilies.

It still has its drawbridge, inner barbican, gatehouse and portcullis grooves. Though much of it has been heavily restored into a Victorian-Tudor structure, there are still the original parts the Badlesmeres knew when they lived there: Edward I's bath, now a boathouse; the famous vineyard where his queen made wine in 1290; some of the towers, and certainly the nearby village church, formerly an ancient priory, dedicated by Crepido Crevecoeur in 1119, its square shape and gaunt tower almost a castle in itself.

The earliest mention of this family is of a Bartholomew de

Badlesmere who in the reign of Henry II was engaged in a law-suit with a William de Cheney over property in Kent, and at about the same time was fined by the king for trespassing in the royal forests, an offence punishable by death to a commoner.

His son William, fighting with the barons against King John, was taken prisoner at Rochester and kept so for over twelve years. His successor, Giles, was killed in a skirmish with the Welsh, and was succeeded by Gunceline de Badlesmere, an even greater rebel than his grandfather. He was so much trouble to Henry III that the king had him excommunicated by the Archbishop of Canterbury, the most dreaded punishment other than death for it forbade burial in consecrated ground. He came back into royal favour, however, and under Edward I fought in the Welsh and French wars with courage and distinction.

He was succeeded by his son, the renowned Bartholomew de Badlesmere, whose short life contained one of the most dramatic episodes in the history of those times. He fought under 'Butcher' Robert de Clifford in Wales, and was appointed Governor of Bristol Castle, two years later being summoned as first baron to Parliament. He is mentioned in the book of the *Siege of Caerlaverock* in 1300 as one of the 400 knights fighting there under Edward I 'Badlesmere who well and bravely bore himself the whole day through'.

Through the influence of the Earls of Gloucester and of Lincoln he was granted, for the duration of his own and his wife's life, the castle and manor of Chilham in Kent. In the fifth year of Edward II's reign, 1312, he was appointed Governor of Leeds Castle in the same county. This was done under a special deed between the king and de Badlesmere in exchange for the latter's manor of Aldrihleye in Shropshire. The king settled the reversion of Leeds Castle upon his queen, Isabella, or so it would appear, all unknowingly touching off yet one more explosion in his already unsettled reign.

Upon the death of 'Butcher' Robert de Clifford, Badlesmere was given the custody of that baron's castle at Skipton, in Yorkshire, to hold during the minority of de Clifford's son and heir.

Badlesmere was now high in royal favour, being granted numerous manors, castles, fairs and markets, and appointed to the stewardship of the royal household. In spite of all this Badlesmere, with many other barons who had first been infuriated by the Gascon favourite Piers Gaveston, and now by the two Despensers who ruled the country through the homosexual king, broke out in open rebellion against him. Under the banner of the Duke of Lancaster they hunted the Despensers like the animals they were, looting and plundering their rich manors and castles all over the country.

It was in October, 1321, when Queen Isabella, on her way to a pilgrimage at Canterbury, suddenly appeared with her retinue before Leeds Castle and demanded hospitality. In the absence of her lord, Lady Badlesmere, through the mouth of her castellan Walter Colepeper, stubbornly refused her admission, saying 'that neither the Queen nor any other should enter without the order of the lord and master'.

The unamiable and hot-tempered queen was stung by what she considered an insulting refusal, and ordered her soldiers to force an entry at once. After a short, sharp attack they were driven off, and in 1822, when excavations were made, six bodies of soldiers were discovered, one with a fractured skull and no feet, obviously killed in the attack.

The infuriated queen was compelled to seek lodging for the night in the nearby Priory of Black Canons, and immediately sent a message to the king informing him of the situation. The unusual alacrity of Edward to raise a force has been suggested by one commentator as an effort to right a wrong, that in fact the castle legally belonged to Isabella and she was merely insisting upon her rights. Reports of this incident are various and confused, the most likely one being that immediately Badlesmere rebelled the king sent his queen to Leeds Castle to occupy it. The king, through his sheriffs, issued urgent summonses to every available man between the ages of sixteen and sixty to assemble under the banner of Aylmer de Valence, Earl of Pembroke, and John de Britannia, Earl of Richmond.

On October 28, at the urgent request of Badlesmere, the Earl
of Hereford and other rebel barons came to Kingston whilst the
Archbishop of Canterbury, the Bishop of London, and the Earl
of Pembroke waited upon the king, requesting him to raise his
proposed siege and let Parliament decide the issue. The king
categorically refused, for further insult had been added, as he said,
by Badlesmere himself addressing a letter to the queen supporting
and confirming Lady Badlesmere's action in refusing to admit
anyone during her lord's absence. The confederate barons, seeing
they were outnumbered, retreated north, and the siege of Leeds
Castle began.

On the 1 November the castle surrendered to the army of
30,000 assembled round its walls, and twelve or thirteen soldiers
were almost immediately hanged, their names being recorded in
the Records Office. In the same year in which excavations discovered soldiers' bodies, a large iron key, that of the castle, was
also found. Since Walter Colepeper had vanished when the castle
gates were opened to the king, it has been assumed that he threw
the key into the moat before swimming across it to escape to his
master in the north.

All Lord Badlesmere's jewels and personal possessions were
taken into custody of the crown, and Lady Badlesmere and her
children sent to the Tower. Shortly after this the barons suffered
a heavy defeat at Boroughbridge, and the exultant king found that
Badlesmere himself had been taken prisoner. He ordered him to
be brought at once to Canterbury, where he was hanged, drawn,
and quartered, and his head stuck upon a pole at Bargate. To re-
mind all traitors that rebellion did not pay Edward ordered some
ninety lords and knights to be similarly treated.

Lady Margaret Badlesmere, herself one of the daughters and
co-heiress of Thomas, third son of Thomas, second son of
Richard de Clare, Earl of Gloucester, remained a prisoner in the
Tower until, through the influence of William, Lord de Roos, she
was released, this Lord de Roos having married her daughter
Margery, the heirs of the marriage later becoming Earls of Rutland.

She at once entered a nunnery near Aldgate in London, receiving two shillings a day for her maintenance there until a substantial portion of the manor belonging to her dead lord was restored to her.

In spite of or because of his father's merciless treatment of the dead baron, Edward III was most gracious to the son, Giles de Badlesmere. He first released him from the Tower, sending a special precept to the Keeper of the Wardrobe there 'to deliver unto the son all his father's harneys, coat-armour as well as other things'. He did not, however, summon him to Parliament for some fifteen years, when he attended as second Baron Badlesmere in 1337, and took livery of all his father's lands with the exception of Leeds Castle, which the king retained for himself.

Giles married Elizabeth, daughter of William de Montacute, the renowned Earl of Salisbury. He died a year later and as there was no male issue the Barony of Badlesmere fell into abeyance between his sisters and co-heiresses, one of whom was Maud, Countess of Oxford, who assumed the barony with no legal right whatsoever.

It remained in the de Vere family for almost 300 years until John de Vere, fourteenth earl, died in 1526, when it once more fell into abeyance between his four sisters.

According to Debrett, Captain Mark Phillips, who married Princess Anne in 1973, can trace royal descent from Elizabeth Badlesmere, who in 1335 married William, Earl of Northampton.

BERKELEY

Arms: Gules, a chevron between ten crosses paty, six in chief and four in base, argent.

Berkeley Castle, in spite of its charming rose-tinted exterior, is the grim and forbidding fortress rather than castle the Normans always built. The twisting passages, narrow doorways and winding staircases were defensible by one or two armed men.

It stands on a mound overlooking the Severn and the beautiful Gloucestershire countryside between Bristol and Gloucester, as formidable a challenge today as when it was first built. William the Conqueror's decree that curfew should be rung here at dusk during the winter months did not cease until the middle of the nineteenth century.

In spite of wars, rebellions, sieges, violence, confiscation and restoration the powerful lords of Berkeley have managed to live in their castle continuously for over 800 years. In recent years since they courteously opened their home to the public, hundreds of thousands of visitors have come to see its furniture, pictures, tapestries, many coats of arms, gardens, and the family church where many of the family lie entombed.

It is one of the remarkable feats of history that they have been able to accomplish this, even to survive at all, and this was undoubtedly due to their great capacity for diplomatic and military skill, shrewdness, cunning, luck and brilliant and wealthy alliances which have highlighted their long and eventful history.

Roger, the original Berkeley, was a leading captain in William the Conqueror's army, for which he received considerable lands in Gloucestershire, and these he bequeathed to his nephew William, founder of the Gloucestershire Abbey of Kingswood. At about this time a small castle had been built by the then powerful lord of the west, William FitzOsbern. He soon saw the strategic importance of Berkeley and at once began to fortify it in the Norman manner. When he went to France he appointed as his representative to hold the castle William de Berkeley's son Roger de Dursley.

In the wars between King Stephen and the Empress Maud, Roger unluckily allied himself with the latter, for which action he suffered terrible punishment. His seeming friend Walter, brother to Milo, Earl of Hereford, treacherously seized him. He was stripped naked, exposed to scorn, put in chains, and thrice drawn up by a rope round his neck to the top of a gallows outside his own castle gates. He was threatened that if he did not deliver up his castle his treatment would be even harsher. When he was almost dead he was carried off and flung into one of his own dungeons to await further torture if he lived.

When Henry II came to the throne he rewarded Roger handsomely, granting him the charter of Berkeley Manor. He had now changed his former name of Dursley to Berkeley, and since those times the Berkeleys have lived in the castle.

There is some confusion here, however, as Henry II granted the lordship of Berkeley Castle to a Robert FitzHardinge in 1153. He was a rich Bristol merchant whose father was the son of a Saxon thane named Eadnoth, who was a 'staller', or household officer, to Edward the Confessor. Eadnoth was one of only two or three Saxons astute enough to ally themselves with the Conqueror. He later fought and died in battle against Harold's rebel sons.

Robert FitzHardinge, whom William of Malmesbury described as 'better used to wag his tongue in strife than to wield his arms in war', at once threw Roger out of the castle and a bitter and bloody feud broke out between the two contestants. The feud only came to an end by the king expeditiously commanding Robert's son Maurice to marry Roger's daughter Alicia. Roger returned to his castle of Dursley and Robert took over Berkeley Castle. Thus Eadnoth's grandson became the first baron and ancestor of the great house of Berkeley down to this day. Robert de Berkeley founded St Augustine's Abbey, now the site of Bristol Cathedral, where he and his wife lie buried in their private chapel, their tombs covered with their own and allied coats of arms.

Robert II, third baron, not only lost the castle but was excommunicated as well for his part in the barons' war against King John. His successor Thomas I is succinctly portrayed by John Smyth, family steward and historian. 'He soe evenly observed a prudent inclyninge after the strongest powers that hee ever avoided these Court and Country stormes which in his time blewe down many stronger Cedars than himself.' This capacity for prudence and agility in assessing situations enabled him to have the castle restored on payment of a heavy fine. His successor, Maurice II, consolidated this still more by marrying the daughter of one of King John's bastards.

When Thomas III succeeded as eighth baron he as skilfully married the daughter of Roger Mortimer, the hated paramour of Isabella, Edward II's wife. It was shortly after that one of the ugliest events in English history took place in Berkeley Castle. This was the callous and brutal murder of the king during Thomas's custodianship of him. Thomas's own father had revolted against the king, had been betrayed and hanged in chains at Wallingford, so that it was all the more surprising, and certainly sinister, that he received Edward 'with much courtesy and kindness'.

The queen and Mortimer had hounded the king from castle to castle. Hired ruffians dragged him from one stinking dungeon filled with rats and rotting corpses, to another. They moved him from Gloucester to Berkeley, to Corfe, and back to Berkeley, but his iron-tough Plantagenet physique still enabled him to keep alive.

On his last grim journey to Berkeley Castle they put a crown of hay on his head, shaved him with stinking ditchwater, and on his arrival at the castle the utterly friendless, homosexual king was flung once more into the dungeon which can be seen today.

His gaolers were two of the most brutal ruffians, Sir Thomas Gurney and Sir John Maltravers. When after five months of harsh captivity orders came from the queen 'for some swift conclusion to the matter', they went to work.

On the night of 21 September 1327 these two thugs carried out a murder unparalleled even in the history of those times. The king was tied face downwards between two mattresses then 'a kind of horn or funnel was thrust into his fundament through which a red-hot spit was run up into his bowels'. His shrieks were heard even beyond the castle walls that dreadful night, and there are people who say they can still be heard there.

His manner of death was chosen no doubt because as a homosexual this would seem to the people to be a justifiable manner of revenge. Instead, however, he became a martyr, and now lies buried in Gloucester Cathedral after his body was refused by the Abbots of Bristol and Malmesbury for fear of the queen's terrible temper and revenge for disobedience.

When Edward III came to the throne Thomas de Berkeley was at once summoned before Parliament to explain his part in the murder. He was able to convince the sovereign, however, that he was absent from his castle that night, and was in fact lying ill at Bradley, some five miles away. He spoke with such conviction that both king and Parliament were sufficiently assured to acquit him. Smyth observes, however, that from all available evidence in the household books his master was most certainly present in the castle.

Thomas de Berkeley IV left an only daughter who married Richard Beauchamp, Earl of Warwick, by whom she had three daughters, the eldest marrying the Earl of Shrewsbury. Warwick, in right of his wife, promptly seized the castle and lands until James, the succeeding nephew could prove his title. At the same time the Earl of Shrewsbury imprisoned James's wife in Gloucester and kept her there until her death.

Sir William, twelfth baron, had honours, lands and titles showered on him. He was created Earl of Nottingham, Baron Mowbray and Segrave, Viscount and Baron Berkeley, and Earl Marshal of England. A furious quarrel broke out between him and the twenty-year-old Viscount Lisle over his father's confiscated lands, the latter sending the former a challenge to 'trial by combat'. They met at Nibley Green in Gloucestershire in 1469, both with small private armies, where the young Lisle was mortally wounded by an arrow shot through his mouth 'his visor being up', for which his young widow later received a pension of £100 a year, the disputed lands being returned to Berkeley. It has been said this was the last private battle to be held in England.

Lord William then had a feud with his brother because of his marriage to the daughter of a mayor of Bristol, for which he was disinherited by William, who accused him 'of unworthiness of a match with so mean blood'. This was conceivably an excuse for Lord William's own unbridled extravagance, and it is even stranger to recall that the original founder of the Berkeley line was himself a Bristol merchant. 'Wasteall' Berkeley, as John Smyth called him, had no children. In return for all his various high privileges, money, honours, and titles, he entailed all his vast estates to Henry VII and thus dispossessed successive Berkeley lords of their lands and castles until after the death of Edward VI in 1553.

'Wasteall's' surviving brother is thus pathetically described by Smyth: 'With his milk white head in his irksome old age of seventy years, with his buckerom bag stuffed with law cases walking with his eldest son Maurice between the Inns of Court and Westminster'. These tireless litigations, however, brought to Maurice after his old father's death, some forty-odd manors. Once again prosperity came to the Berkeley family.

Henry, seventeenth baron, was a mighty hunter. He was absent when Queen Elizabeth and her adored Earl of Leicester visited Berkeley Castle. As she also had a passion for hunting she caused such havoc and slaughter that Henry, receiving news of this, at once sent back a messenger with orders 'to have the lands disparked'. Elizabeth as promptly sent the messenger back reminding Henry 'to be very careful as my Lord of Leicester greatly desireth the castle for himself'.

During the Civil Wars Berkeley Castle was damaged, but repairs were carried out by George 'The Harmless', as he was called. His love of ease and culture brought him the friendship of Robert Burton, who dedicated his *Anatomy of Melancholy* to him. George's son, also George, was created Viscount Dursley and first Earl of Berkeley.

In the lifetime of Frederick Augustus, fifth earl, a strange event took place which directly affected the continuing lineage of the Berkeley line. This earl was not only a great rake and gambler, but also a murderer, having one day callously shot dead a local highwayman. He shortly after seduced Mary Cole, the daughter of a respectabl local tradesman, and took her to live with him at the Castle as 'Mary Tudor'.

After producing a litter of no less than eight children, the earl took her to Lambeth and married her. She had no sooner achieved that status than she demanded he should force, or persuade, the local priest to issue a certificate of marriage dated back to the time of her seduction, in order to legitimate the eight bastards.

A certificate was accordingly produced 'in very strange circumstances', and in 1710, when the earl died, his eldest son, the Viscount Dursley, petitioned his claim to the title before the House of Lords, and so began the celebrated Berkeley Peerage Case.

The certificate of the first marriage was found to be 'not proven', and his claim to the title therefore refused on account of his illegitimacy. He was, however, allowed to keep all the lands and castle, and was created Baron Segrave of Berkeley and Earl FitzHardinge. As he died leaving no issue these titles became extinct.

The present owner of the castle Major R. J. G. Berkeley is twenty-fourth in lineal descent from the first Robert Fitz-Hardinge, to whom Berkeley Castle was granted by Henry II over 800 years ago in 1153.

BROCAS

Arms: Sable, a lion rampant guardant or.

There can be few great English families who have left behind
them as much abundant evidence of their former existence as that
of de Brocas.

In the Tower of London armoury is the famous fifteenth-century
tilting helmet known as the Brocas Helm. It is considered by ex-
perts to be the finest example of its kind, still having its original
staples and locking bars, back and front, for fastening it down
securely on the chest and shoulders and weighs 22½lb.

There are splendid canopied tombs in St Edmund's Chapel,
Westminster Abbey, near to the royal tombs, in the Hampshire
churches of Sherborne St John and Bramley and in the Surrey
churches of St Nicholas, Guildford, and Peper Harow near
Godalming. There are also in Sherborne St John church some of
the finest engraved monumental brasses to be seen in England,
depicting the head-dresses, costume, arms, armour and tabards of
the various periods of the family history. On the roof of Bramley
church are the weather vanes bearing the Moor's head crest.

About a mile away to the south-west stands Beaurepaire, the family home for almost six generations.

Though now almost completely destroyed after several damaging wars and fires, it stands in extensive parkland surrounded by the original moat, over which are narrow bridges entered by wrought-iron gates between gate piers imposingly surmounted by the Moor's head crest.

Unlike so many other famous families who, often erroneously, claim descent from, or prior to, the Norman Conquest, that of de Brocas did not appear in English history until about 1312. In that year, Arnauld, head of the line, came over from Beaurepaire, in Gascony—hence the name of the family mansion in Hampshire—and was killed at Bannockburn in 1314. They had, nevertheless, been known to Edward I long before as 'that clan of Gascon gentlemen'.

The family had always been loyal to the English kings in their constant wars with the French, and Arnauld was thus well received in the court of Edward II, who together with his country, was completely dominated and ruled by another Gascon, the infamous Piers de Gaveston, the most hated and despised man in England, who was finally caught, degraded, and executed by the barons who rose against him and his homosexual and besotted sovereign, their hatred of him exceeding even his for them.

A further reason for de Brocas being welcome was the fact that the Gascons were noted for their skill in horse-breeding, so that after the death of Arnauld his three sons became royal wards, and on the brutal murder of Edward II in 1327, his son, Edward III, appointed John, the eldest of the three brothers as Master of the King's Horse. Edward III was not only a splendid horseman himself, but a very fine judge of their quality, and was prepared to back his judgement by spending vast sums of money for a proved thoroughbred. He once spent the huge sum, in those days, of £2,500 for an Irish-bred horse, and several times paid £1,000 for one.

This John was the real founder of the Brocas line in England. He also did much to make Windsor what it is today, since he was

not only appointed Governor but employed by the king in building the fortifications of the great castle, for which service he was
knighted as Sir John de Brocas of Clewer and Windsor. He was
also appointed an officer of the royal household. The first recorded
family document granted him and his wife a small property in
Windsor. As a reward for his military service in France he was
granted a penny in the pound on all silver coinage minted in the
king's duchy of Aquitaine.

Sir John's third and youngest brother was a soldier priest who
was also rector of Guildford, Keeper of the Royal Parks, Constable of Guildford Castle, and later of Bordeaux Castle, for all of
which services he was granted vast estates in Surrey and Hampshire. He it was who bought Cockerell Hulle in 1353, for 100
silver marks, changing its name to Beaurepaire and bequeathing
it to his nephew, where it continued to remain in the family for
six generations of descendants.

Sir John had three sons and it was the third, Sir Bernard, who
became the shining star in the family firmament. He was born in
1330, rapidly distinguishing himself as a fine soldier, and certainly
fought at Crécy and Poitiers. He was a cousin and boon com-
panion of the Black Prince, being of the same age, and after the
prince's death he was chosen as a special guest to attend the
funeral. Like his father, Sir Bernard was actively engaged in the
rebuilding of Windsor Castle, thus coming into contact with the
great William of Wykeham, Lord Chancellor, equal almost in
power to John of Gaunt himself, with whom he was constantly
engaged in political struggles.

Upon William's enthronement as Bishop of Winchester, Sir
Bernard was one of three selected knights to be personally invited.
The bishop later made him sovereign warden and surveyor of the
parks 'throughout our bishopric'. He also sat in Parliament, once
for Wiltshire and ten times for Hampshire.

In addition to all his own vast lands and estates he had now
inherited, through his uncle the rector of Guildford, the mansion
of Beaurepaire in Hampshire. He at once set about making it one
of the most splendid houses in the country, and was shortly

granted the very high privilege of receiving licence to empark and crenellate it.

Upon the death of Edward III and the accession to the throne of Richard II, Sir Bernard continued in high and royal favour. He was appointed Captain of Calais, the most important office to be held outside England. When Richard married Anne of Bohemia Sir Bernard became her Chamberlain.

He was married three times, gaining materially in each case. At the age of twenty-four he married firstly Agnes, daughter of Sir Mauger Vavasour. She brought as her dowry several rich manors and estates in the north of England. She seems to have had vagaries, for a young Bernard appeared on the scene which she found not easy to explain to her husband, and the six-year marriage ended in divorce. She re-married almost at once but it was some considerable time before she got any of her dowry estates back from her former husband, who was generous enough to return them in the end.

Sir Bernard next played his highest matrimonial card by courting Lady Joan Plantagenet, the Fair Maid of Kent, encouraged in his pursuit of the coveted prize by the Black Prince himself. Though not successful in his suit he was completely undeterred, as in all his undertakings, switching his attentions to Mary de Borhunte, the extremely wealthy heiress to the Anglo-Norman family of des Roches, and collaterally descended from Peter de Rupibus, Bishop of Winchester.

Mary des Roches, whom he married in 1361, not only brought him manors and estates all over the country but, through the ancient manor of Weldon, near Uppingham, Rutland, the hereditary Mastership of the Royal Buckhounds, a highly valued and privileged office which remained in the Brocas family for some 300 years.

Mary died after twelve years of marriage and he gave estates and lands to Clewer and Windsor and built chantries to her memory. These things accomplished, he married for the third time in 1382, a rich widow, Katherine, upon the death of her husband Sir Hugh Tyrrell. He seems now to have settled to the life of the wealthy country squire he was, hunting with his buckhounds, supervising his estates and the constant building of the family mansion which was, even then, one of the finest in the land.

He died in 1395 and was buried with great pomp and ceremony in St Edmund's Chapel, Westminster Abbey, close to the royal tombs. His richly decorated monument carries the Brocas arms and the crest which tradition says 'was for overcoming the King of Morocco and cutting off his head'. This was described by Addison in one of his essays in *The Spectator* when the Abbey verger pointed out the tomb to Sir Roger de Coverley, who was much moved by the story. The crest was found on the seal of Sir Bernard as early as 1361, the date of his second marriage, he being the first to use it, and the Brocas arms were impaled with the arms of des Roches, *sable, two lions passant guardant or*. This crest was the result of some probable feat of chivalry in the reign of Edward III, and has been used by the Brocas descendants ever since.

He was succeeded by the son of his second marriage, another Sir Bernard, who also held high offices under Richard II. It is this son whom Shakespeare put into his play *The Tragedy of King Richard the Second*. Sir Bernard was as loyal and devoted a servant as his father was to Richard II throughout the troubled years of that king's uneasy reign, and he most bitterly opposed the seizure of the crown by the usurping Henry IV. He at once entered a conspiracy to restore Richard to the throne, and Froissart has painted a graphic picture of the results of his failure to carry out his ambitious plan.

Richard was a prisoner in the Tower after reigning for twenty-two years. The Duke of Lancaster, with a chosen body of counsellors, went to him there and read out a complete indictment of his reign 'to which the king made no reply'. The duke then returned to Guildhall and read the indictment aloud to an angry crowd demanding revenge and justice, for the king had divulged the names of his four counsellors to the murders of Gloucester, Arundel and Sir Thomas Corbet, in the hope that such a betrayal would save his own life. The crowd demanded their names, also that the king should be confined to prison on bread and water for the rest of his miserable life.

As the demands for justice on the counsellors of the murders calculatedly increased, the duke withdrew to the judgement chamber before returning to inform the crowd that the four knights were condemned to death. Their names were Lord Marclois, Sir John Derby (receiver of Lincoln), Lord Stelle (steward of the household) and Sir Bernard Brocas.

The four knights were tied by their feet to horses and dragged from the Tower through the streets of London to Cheapside, where their heads were cut off on a fishmonger's slab. Another version of their deaths states that they were beheaded at Tyburn and that Sir Bernard's last words were: 'Thank God that I was born for I shall die this night in the service of the noble king Richard'. The date in both cases is agreed as 4 February 1400. Shakespeare's record of the death of Sir Bernard is totally inaccurate.

This 'dark conspiracy', as it was called, not only resulted in Sir Bernard's death but in the forfeiture of all his vast estates, including Beaurepaire. These, however, were later restored to his son William. The family had always been very astute about money, properties, and settlements, especially when, about this time, another Bernard married Emeline Sandys of The Vyne, quite near to Beaurepaire. It is an historic house of great beauty, now the property of the National Trust and open to the public. In spite of the forfeiture there is no evidence that Beaurepaire was ever taken over; indeed, four more generations continued to live there.

Throughout the Wars of the Roses the Brocas family was divided. One side held The Vyne for the Yorkists, and another held Beaurepaire for the Lancastrians, though the latter was very severely damaged.

The third and last William died in 1506, leaving two daughters, joint co-heiresses to the title and fortune. Upon the death of Anne, Edith became sole heiress, bringing her vast wealth, and Beaurepaire, to Ralph Pexall. The son of this marriage, Sir Richard Pexall Brocas, became so notorious that his name became synonymous with lechery. He was said to have fathered more than 100 bastards during his rakish and dissolute life. He preferred not to live at Beaurepaire, going instead to Steventon, another family manor in Hampshire, which had once cost a Brocas £20,000 and is now derelict.

He very soon began to sell some of the family estates to pay for his chosen way of life, and during the last years of Elizabeth's reign was forced to seek her royal pardon for the curiously mixed offences of riot and forgery. His notorious way of life continued, however, and he was finally summoned to the Court of High Commission under King James I and sentenced to do public penance. Stowe reports in his *History of England*: 'Sir Ralph Pecsall Brocas did open penance at St Paul's Cross. He stood in a white sheete, and held a stick in his hand, having been formally convicted by the High Commissioners for secret and notorious adulteries with divers women.'

Sir Pexall Brocas, having completed his penance, went with thirty of his retainers, all dressed in scarlet, to Guildhall, insolently demanding 'a dinner from the Lord Mayor after doing the required penance'. It is not recorded if a meal was forthcoming; nor is it known how or why he ever received a knighthood; nor why he was refused a high place at the coronation of James I after claiming the privilege as hereditary Master of the Buck-hounds. In a final attempt to redeem himself he drew up his will, leaving £4,000 to the University of Oxford for the foundation of a new college to be called Brocas College. This last burst of philanthropy, however, seems not to have brought results.

During the Civil Wars, when once again different branches of the family fought on opposite sides, old Thomas Brocas staked everything on a Royalist victory, and after the defeat of Charles he was completely ruined. In 1656 he was imprisoned for debt, nearly all his estates being sold to satisfy his creditors. Beaurepaire was saved only because his son Thomas had fought with the Parliamentary army and had enough influence with Cromwell to save it from confiscation. Successive members of the family held it until about 1873 when it became a financial liability. The family was forced to sell the house, as the result of which Bernard Brocas, then the owner, committed suicide through grief.

On 14 October 1819, Samuel Jellicoe married Jane Elizabeth, first daughter of Sir James Whalley-Smythe-Gardiner, second baronet, who claimed lineal descent from the Brocas family through the marriage of Jane Brocas, the then legal heir at law, with Sir William Gardiner.

Over a century later, in 1925, a grateful Parliament granted Viscount Jellicoe of Scapa, Co Orkney, £50,000 for outstanding service to the nation. He was further created Earl Jellicoe and, in full recognition of the claim made by his ancestors to the family name, Viscount Brocas of Southampton, Co Southampton.

BROWNE

Viscounts Montagu

Arms: Sable, three lions passant in bend between two double cotises argent.

There are few more picturesque and impressive ruins in England than those of Cowdray at Midhurst in Sussex. It was completely gutted by fire in 1793 as the result of a curse put upon the Montagu family some 250 years earlier at the Dissolution of the Monasteries, when the monks were thrown out of their Abbey at Battle.

Legend has it that when Sir Anthony Browne occupied Battle Abbey in Sussex, granted to him by Henry VIII, he held high revelry there and grossly insulted the monks before driving them out. As the last monk reached the door he turned and uttered the famous Cowdray Curse 'That the house of the despoiler of the Abbey should perish utterly by fire and water'.

The ruins are reached from the main street of Midhurst by a causeway running eastwards for a quarter of a mile, as bare and gaunt as the ruins themselves. This once splendid Elizabethan mansion, mainly built by the Earl of Southampton about 1530, still has some fine remnants, including the great bay with sixty openings, the fine vaulted brickwork roof of the tiled cellar floor, the north and south porches with traces of original plaster-work and fan-vaulted stone ceiling, and the chapel.

In the south chapel of Easebourne church, near Midhurst, are family tombs and effigies. On a marble and alabaster altar tomb are two richly costumed female figures. Above this tomb stands another, where a bearded knight in gilt armour kneels before an altar. These effigies, dated 1593, are of Sir Anthony Browne, 1st Viscount Montagu, KG, together with his two wives, Lady Jane Ratcliffe, daughter of the Earl of Sussex, and Magdalen, daughter of William, Lord Dacre. On the south wall are two fine marble monuments to Mr and Mrs Poyntz, upon whom the Cowdray curse finally fell.

The head of the line, Sir Anthony Browne, was created Knight of the Bath at the coronation of King Richard II. Of his two sons the younger was Sir Stephen Browne, who as Lord Mayor of London imported large cargoes of rye from Prussia at a time of a great shortage of wheat, and distributed it to the poor people of London.

His grandson, Sir Thomas, of Beechworth Castle, Surrey, was Henry VI's Household Treasurer and made a distinguished marriage with Eleanor, daughter and co-heiress of Sir Thomas Fitz-Alan and niece of John, Earl of Arundel. He was, however, beheaded during the reign of Richard III.

Almost fifty years later his descendant was Anthony, who, in the first year of the reign of Henry VII had been given the high appointment of Standard Bearer 'for the whole realm of England and elsewhere'. He was next given the Governorship of Queenborough Castle, Kent, and was knighted in 1486 for his share in the victory over the Earl of Lincoln and Lambert Simnel at Newark. He married Lucy, fourth daughter and co-heiress of John Nevill, Marquess of Montagu.

His son, Sir Anthony Browne, was with the Lord High

Admiral at Southampton for the preparations connected with Henry VIII's journey to Biscay, convoying the monarch from that port. He was knighted for his gallantry in the assault he made on Morleis in Brittany. During the minority of the Earl of Derby he was appointed Lieutenant of the Isle of Man. He next held the office of Master of the Horse, but more important still, he was, after the Dissolution of the Monasteries, granted the estates and monastery of Battle in Sussex, made a Knight of the Garter, and appointed one of the executors of the king's will. He was also granted the highly privileged position his father had held as Standard Bearer to the sovereign.

His son, Sir Anthony, was created first Viscount Montagu by Queen Mary in 1554, and made a Knight of the Garter, but on the accession of Queen Elizabeth his name was left out of the Privy Council, and being a fervent Catholic he voted against the abolition of Papal supremacy. Elizabeth, nevertheless, 'having experienced his loyalty had great esteem of him', and paid him the honour of a visit. This was in gratitude for his action when a very old man, England being threatened by the Armada, in journeying to Tilbury with his sons, grandson, and twenty of his best friends to offer service to Her Majesty, in spite of the fact that he was a Roman Catholic.

Before this time, however, in the year 1530, the Earl of Southampton had begun to build the magnificent Tudor house of Cowdray. He died childless in 1543 and the whole estate came to Sir Anthony Browne, his half-brother, who completed the building of what was thought to be one of the finest houses in England, and furnished it with wonderful treasures.

It was here that Queen Elizabeth visited Viscount Montagu in the summer of 1591, staying for one week. She did not arrive until the evening and then with an immense retinue, the cost of her visits very often bankrupting her hosts. She went to bed early after the prolonged and elaborate welcomes given her. For breakfast the next morning no less than three oxen and 140 geese were consumed, and she, no doubt, drank her usual full measure of ale.

31

She then rode into the great park and 'skilfully shot' three or four deer carefully steered into her range of fire, following which she mounted one of the towers to watch sixteen bucks pulled down by greyhounds on the lawn. The programme continued through the next day, and on the third she hunted. She was then in her fifty-ninth year, tough and intrepid as ever. The expenses for her hospitality were almost ruinous.

The third viscount, Francis, suffered much in the Civil Wars, but survived to see the restoration of the monarchy. He married Elizabeth, youngest daughter of Henry Somerset, Marquess of Worcester. His son Francis succeeded him, and being a staunch Catholic, was appointed Lord Lieutenant of Sussex by James II. He married the daughter of William Herbert, Marquess of Powys. As he died childless the succession passed to his brother Henry.

It was when George-Samuel Browne inherited as eighth viscount that the full prophesied tragedy struck down the house of Montagu. In 1794 the viscount's sister Elizabeth Mary married William Stephen Poyntz of Midgham, Berkshire, a descendant of the ancient Poyntz family of Iron Acton in Gloucestershire. Just before the marriage the young viscount, twenty-five years of age and himself betrothed, travelled to Switzerland with his friend Sedley Burdet to shoot the rapids at Schaffhausen in a flat-bottomed boat. The local magistrate, learning of such a dangerous and foolhardy undertaking, not only forbade it but had guards posted to prevent it.

The two friends succeeded in eluding the guards, however, and pushed off in their boat, successfully shooting the first fall. At their attempt to clear the second fall disaster struck them, and they and their boat totally disappeared, both young men being drowned. The young viscount's body was recovered from the water and is said to be buried at Laufenburg.

While this tragedy was taking place Mr and Mrs Poyntz had gone for their honeymoon, leaving workmen in Cowdray Park preparing for the return and marriage of the young viscount. It was but a few days before the Poyntzes were urgently sent for to find the magnificent Elizabethan house almost completely gutted by fire.

Workmen had apparently left some smouldering rubbish in the north gallery which rapidly spread flames through the house. Everything then seemed to assist the destruction. There was a very high wind, almost a gale, blowing and the key of the engine house was lost. All that was preserved was the keeper's lodge in the park, where the Poyntzes were forced to live.

They at once sent a messenger to Schaffhausen with news of the tragedy urging the viscount to return immediately. At Calais this messenger met another coming from Schaffhausen, bearing news of his death by drowning to his sister. Only then was the 'Cowdray Curse' recalled, but it had not yet completed its course.

Almost twenty-two years later Mr and Mrs Poyntz and their two sons were on holiday in Bognor. It was a perfect summer day and Mr Poyntz decided to take his two sons out in a boat in spite of his wife's anxiety about the curse, which was still fresh in their minds. He had not been long away when a freak storm came from nowhere, capsized the boat and almost immediately drowned the boys. He himself was only rescued at the last moment by a fishermen who had been unable to save the others.

Six months later Mr Poyntz was thrown from his horse while hunting and never fully recovered from the concussion he received. In 1830 he had had the nuns' church of Easebourne Priory rebuilt as a memorial chapel to the Browne and Poyntz families, at the same time converting the wall of the dais end of the refectory into a most unusual pigeon-house to accommodate more than a thousand pigeons.

In 1908 the Cowdray estates were sold to Sir Weetman Dickinson Pearson, Bart, who became the first Viscount Cowdray. He restored the ruins to their existing fine state of preservation. His descendant is the present Viscount Cowdray of Cowdray and Baron Cowdray of Midhurst, both in Sussex, and a baronet.

COURTENAY

Earls of Devon

Arms: Or, three torteaux and a label of three points azure.

Though not easily visible from much of the surrounding Devon-shire countryside, Powderham Castle, eight miles south-west of Exeter, and visited annually by some 40,000 tourists, still stands guard over the Exe estuary.

Its once vast estates of 50,000 acres have shrunk to 3,000, and most of its medieval structure disappeared in the Civil Wars when terrible damage was inflicted on it by the Parliamentary troops.

Here, for almost 600 years, the members of the extant and collateral line of the house of Courtenay have lived. Sir Philip Courtenay rebuilt it in 1390, retaining some of the original struc-ture put up by Isabel de Fortibus, herself a daughter of the original Earls of Devon, almost a century earlier.

The senior line, however, always lived at Tiverton, where they had another great castle on the Exe and considerable lands and manors. They wielded formidable power in the west country by

34

their ability to summon at once an army of 4,000 foot soldiers and 800 cavalry. Their power was solidly built on their inherited Norman aggression and arrogance. They acknowledged no higher authority than the king and not always him. Once, in an angry outburst against the Mayor of Exeter, they promptly cut off the town's important sea trade by building weirs across the Exe which flowed through their lands, and began to build up Topsham into the prosperity it enjoys even today.

Not far from Powderham Castle stands the little church of St Clement, fortified by Cromwell whose troops irretrievably damaged the tombs. Here fourteen women and twelve men of the Courtenay family lie buried. The great and comfortable family pew is itself a remarkable thing and the Courtenay arms are everywhere to be seen, even on pews and bench ends, and many splendid armorial windows with shields quartering their numerous alliances. A medieval weather vane on the tower has the figure of a dolphin which was one of the Courtenay devices of the Byzantine Empire.

One interesting coat of arms is that of Courtenay impaled with Bonville. This was to commemorate the marriage of Sir William Courtenay to Margaret, daughter of Lord Bonville, and obviously a final measure taken to end the years of bitter and bloody feuds between the rich rival families over the stewardship of Devon, which caused misery to that county for years, finally ending in the execution of Lord Bonville and the family's disappearance from history.

This very illustrious and ancient family, of which Gibbon has written a short but brilliant account in his *Decline and Fall of the Roman Empire*, descended from Athon, a wealthy French knight, who lived in the year 1000. He built the great castle of Courtenay in the Gatinois district of France, some fifty-six miles south of Paris, from which the family took its name. His grandson was the famous crusader Joscelin of Courtenay who became Count of Edessa on the Euphrates, and died in 1131. His nephew Renaud, or Reginald, was expelled by Louis VII, and took refuge in England. Louis VII at the same time married his own son Peter to

Reginald's sister, and their son, Peter de Courtenay, was elected Emperor of Constantinople in 1216, two years before his death. Two successive members of the family were also emperors.

When Reginald fled to England, accompanying Henry II's queen Eleanor, he was granted lands and estates in Berkshire at Sutton, now Sutton Courtenay, and founded the great English senior line which later split into cadet lines and the extant collateral line at Powderham through a series of brilliant marriages with other great families such as de Vere, Despencer, St John, de Bohun, Camoys, Talbot, Beaufort, and even the great Plantagenets themselves.

The part they played in English history is truly astonishing and Burke's remark that 'the wonder is not that these families existed but that they survived at all' could not be truer. Again and again they were threatened with extinction for though of Yorkist blood they were staunch and loyal Lancastrians. At one time no less than three successive brothers died, one after another, in the Lancastrian cause, two of them by beheading. Their lands and honours were more than once forfeited and restored. They were killed in battle. They were imprisoned. Among their descendants were three bishops—of Norwich, London and Exeter—and one Archbishop of Canterbury, 'that haughty prelate' as Shakespeare called him in *Richard III*. They were Chancellors of Oxford. Peter, when Bishop of Exeter, brought to the cathedral the great bell, weighing 12,500lb, still called 'Peter's Bell', as well as completing the north tower of the cathedral, at his own cost.

On the death of the head of the line, Sir Reginald de Courtenay, in 1194 he was succeeded by his son Robert as feudal Baron of Okehampton, Governor of the castles of Exeter, Bridgnorth, and Oxford, and was granted by King John the rich concession of the coinage of the tin in Devonshire and Cornwall. He married the daughter of William Redvers, the sixth original Earl of Devon, who brought him very great estates, including Tiverton, where the senior line settled.

His great-grandson Hugh was created first Earl of Devon and summoned to Parliament by Edward III as Hugh de Courtenay

Earl of Devon, the first in that order and in right of his great-grandmother. He was succeeded by his son Hugh, who became the second earl and brought off a dazzling marriage by taking as his bride the aristocratic and autocratic Margaret de Bohun, daughter of the Earl of Hereford and Essex, and granddaughter of Edward I. With characteristic medieval fertility and vigour she presented Hugh with no less than eight sons and nine daughters.

Of the sons, three were outstanding; William the fourth son who became Archbishop of Canterbury, Philip the sixth, who founded the present Courtenay line of Powderham Castle which he rebuilt, and Peter the seventh, who was Standard Bearer to Edward III, Governor of Windsor Castle and Chamberlain to Richard II. William, an implacable enemy of the Lollards, became Archbishop of Canterbury when his predecessor was murdered. He was also Chancellor of Oxford.

He seems to have had much of the arrogance of the more military side of the family and was once nearly killed in his own cathedral of St Paul's by the all powerful John of Gaunt at the trial of Wycliffe. He also fell out badly with the Bishop of Exeter, whom he threatened with excommunication. The Bishop's men had caught one of Courtenay's emissaries with a message to their master and forced him to eat it, wax, seal, and all. When the matter reached the king's ears he was furious and threatened to deprive the bishop of his temporal powers.

Courtenay was unhappily chosen to reprove Richard II for his evil ways, telling him that unless he ruled differently he would ruin himself and the country. The king reacted with all his known and much feared violence, and only his uncle, Thomas of Wood-stock prevented him from laying hands on the Archbishop. Courtenay, under threat of deprivation of all his offices, took refuge in Devon, but at the start of his journey was hotly pursued to the Thames by the king himself. Courtenay was forced to disguise himself in a monk's habit to escape.

Edward, the third earl, who succeeded his grandfather, was known as the 'Blind Earl'. If he was in fact blind, as Gibbon asserts, it is difficult to reconcile this with Burke's statement that he was admiral of all the king's fleet from the mouth of the Thames westward. 'But the good Earl thus speaks from the tomb', wrote Gibbon: ' "What we gave we have. What we spent we had. What we left we lost" '—as fair a summing-up of the Courtenay fortunes as any that could be made, even by such a brilliant historian as Gibbon.

Thomas, the fifth earl, who married Margaret Beaufort, John of Gaunt's granddaughter, died while travelling to London on a mission of mediation to the king and was buried in Abingdon Abbey. His three sons died tragically. Thomas, the sixth earl and his brother the seventh earl were both beheaded. The third brother, the eighth earl was killed at the battle of Tewkesbury. With the death of these three all the honours of the senior line of Courtenay fell under attainder but were restored by Henry VII to Sir Edward, great-great-grandson of the second earl, Hugh, who had married Margaret de Bohun.

Sir Edward's son, Sir William, made the second royal marriage which once again brought the Courtenays dangerously near to the throne. His bride was Lady Katherine Plantagenet, sixth daughter of Edward IV and sister of Henry VII's queen, Elizabeth. Accused by Henry VII of being in traitorous correspondence with Edmund de la Pole, Earl of Suffolk, Sir William was arrested and sent to the Tower, and once again the honours were forfeited. When Henry VIII came to the throne he restored them, but Sir William died before having either letters patent or formal restoration of the earldom, though by royal command he was given all the funeral honours of an earl.

His son Henry was restored in blood and honours as second Earl of Devon of the new creation, and later made Marquess of Exeter. He was high in royal favour, being first cousin to the king. He played an active part firstly in the divorce of Katherine of Aragon and secondly in the trial of Anne Boleyn. He was granted considerable lands in Devon and Cornwall, where his rule was supreme enough for him to take an independent attitude towards Thomas Cromwell, whom he loathed. As grandson of

Edward IV he had a certain claim to the throne and Cromwell was not slow to point this out to the king as a grave danger.

The Marquess's second wife was a devout Catholic, which did nothing to placate either Cromwell or his master, and spies were sent to Devon to collect evidence against him. The king's furious jealousy of Reginald Pole, Dean of Exeter, soon led him to accuse Courtenay, Nevill, and Montacute of conspiring to put the Dean on the throne, and all three were summarily beheaded on Tower Hill. Yet once more the family honours and titles of Courtenay were forfeited, and there was a melancholy note in their former motto *Ubi lapsus? Quod feci?*—'Where have I fallen? What shall I do?'

His son Edward, when only twelve, was imprisoned in the Tower, spending no less than fifteen years there, many of them in solitary confinement, before being released by Mary, when she became Queen of England. As first Earl of Devon of the new creation he carried the sword of state at her coronation. Neither she, nor Elizabeth later, were blind to the qualities of this agreeable, dissolute, exceedingly handsome young man, tall, with a long auburn beard and hair, who spoke many languages, though long years in prison had robbed him of much good breeding and made him unstable and unreliable. Such affection had Mary for him that she did not let him out of her sight, even ordering him to accept no invitations to dinner without her knowledge or permission. Rumours were soon rife that he hoped to marry her and he kept a princely household, even forcing his retainers to kneel to him, but her marriage to Philip of Spain altered everything. His jealous fury was mitigated only by the affection Princess Elizabeth now showed him, and his close advisers urged him to make some move towards a proposal of marriage.

The people were by now restless under a Spanish king and a religion they bitterly hated, and a plot to dethrone both him and Mary began with the pledged support of Devon and Cornwall under the command of Carew. Wyatt undertook to raise the men of Kent, and it was the failure of his too premature rebellion which exposed the whole plot. Though Courtenay had been given command to suppress Wyatt's rebellion he was accused of being an accessory to the plot, and both he and the Princess Elizabeth were imprisoned in the Tower, Courtenay subsequently in Fotheringhay, though they were later released by Philip of Spain, who showed singular mercy towards his sworn enemies in religion.

Courtenay, no longer able to continue his former dissolute way of life, with the prospect of a possible royal marriage, asked and was granted by the queen permission to go abroad, first to France where he was still a virtual prisoner under her orders, and then to Italy. He died in Padua in 1556, not unsuspected of being poisoned. As he was unmarried the senior male line became extinct and was in abeyance for 265 years.

The Courtenays now continued to exist through the collateral and extant line of Powderham founded by Sir Philip, though with lesser honours and titles, being only viscounts. As true Royalists they once more faced extinction when the Civil War broke out and they held Powderham Castle for the king. The Roundheads did fearful damage to both the castle and the church, bringing them to the verge of bankruptcy, but once again they came through with that indomitable courage and large measure of fortune and luck that seemed always to be supporting them.

It was not until 1830, however, that the strangest event of all in their family history brought them once again into the limelight they had always enjoyed. This was when William, third viscount of the Powderham line, made an important, even vital discovery when researching through his family history. This was the governing clause of succession in the creation of the earldom granted to Earl Edward who had died in Padua leaving the title in abeyance for 265 years.

The limit to the succession was stated simply as 'heirs male' and not, as was customary, 'heirs male of the body'. He immediately consulted the Attorney General and took his appeal to the House of Lords. The case was irrefutable and his right to the re-establishment of the earldom was granted although James I, who considered it vacant, had given it to the Cavendish family, now Dukes of Devonshire.

Thus Edward's nearest heir (since he had no issue, being un-married) was a sixth cousin twice removed, who became *de jure* second earl, and all successive earls *de jure* from the date of William's claim. He himself, therefore, became ninth Earl of Devon, but as he also died unmarried the Viscountcy of Courtenay became extinct and the earldom and baronetcy devolved upon his cousin William, tenth Earl of Devon, and has continued down to the present day.

The arms of these earls are: *Quarterly; 1 and 4 or, three torteaux*, for Courtenay; *2 and 3 or, a lion rampant azure*, for Redvers (the original Earls of Devon).

DISNEY

Arms: Argent, on a fess gules three fleurs-de-lis or.

Though their former great castle and manor house have completely disappeared in the little Lincolnshire village of Norton Disney, there are enough monuments in the church the Disneys founded and built to keep their name alive for ever as landmarks in the history of the village bearing their name.

To this quiet corner of England on the wooded banks of the little river Witham come many Americans, descendants of the family cadet line of which, for them, the most illustrious member was Walt Disney, born in Chicago in 1901, lived in Los Angeles, and died on 15 December 1966, creator of such immortal films as *Mickey Mouse* and *Snow White and the Seven Dwarfs*, as well as many others which have brought joy into the hearts of millions of people throughout the world.

There before them in the beautiful church of St Peter, are the five splendid stone effigies of members of the family, three of them women, and above them the quite remarkable early sixteenth-century Disney palimpsest, or reversed brass, one of the finest to be seen in England and unique of its kind. The first effigy on the floor, lying in a recess, is the lovely figure of Joan d'Iseney, granddaughter of Sir Peter de Amundevil of the nearby village and Disney manor of Kingerby, as Kinkerby was then called. She lies in a coif and wimple, a collared and chained dog at her feet. She was quite probably the foundress of the church about the year 1300, since the position of her place in the church usually indicated this.

The second figure, on a coffin-shaped tomb, dated about 1350, is that of Joan, wife of William Disney, a feudal lord, and daughter of Nicholas de Langford. She has jewels in her hair, her hands folded in prayer, and a dog at her feet. The third is of their daughter Hautacia as appears from the Norman lettering on the slab and is probably late fourteenth century. There are shields on the coping of the stone.

There are two other effigies of knights in armour, one on an altar tomb, probably that of Sir William Disney, husband of the Joan mentioned above, and of the same date. Another knight lies under a canopy with a shield.

The monumental heraldic wall brass is framed in oak and joined to show the palimpsest, or reverse side, of an original Flemish brass of 1518, the completion of which may be seen on another brass in the church of West Lavington, Wiltshire. It is divided into five compartments, and the details on the brass are almost overwhelming. The Disney arms, impaling those of William Disney's first wife Margaret Joiner, head the whole design. There are also the arms of Hussey and Ayscough, with crests of Disney and Hussey.

There are engraved figures of Richard Disney and his two wives with their seven sons and five daughters. William Disney, helmeted and in armour kneels opposite Margaret Joiner. Their hands are clasped in prayer over the fauld stool between them, on which lie open books. Behind him are ranked their four sons; behind her their five daughters. The most curiously interesting thing about the whole brass is the entirely modern look about the half armoured, helmeted knights. They all have youthful, smiling faces and are bearded, moustached, and bewhiskered. Some of the sons' names are eliminated because, it was said, though without reliable evidence, their father's will had been in dispute.

There are other Disney monuments in the nearby villages of Kinkerby and Swinderby, former family manors, and Eastgate Place, Lincoln, known as Disney Place. In Ingatestone church in Essex there is a wall monument to an Edgar Norton Disney, of the Swinderby and The Hyde junior line, on which is a shield completely covered with quarterings.

Though the Disney family had great religious and cultural influence over all the people in this ancient farming community, and made wealthy alliances with other noble families, they did not distinguish themselves to any high degree; indeed, their origin was very humble. Unlike most of the great Norman invaders, who were men of wealth and position in their own country before coming over with William the Conqueror to enrich themselves still more, Lambert Disney, acknowledged head of the English line, was very far from being a nobleman. He was probably an adventurer, and unpaid mercenary soldier, attracted by the prospect of loot and plunder, seeing in the invasion of England a rare opportunity to improve his chances of rich rewards.

The original family name was d'Isigny or d'Eisney, from the little village near Bayeux in Normandy, and later became softened into Disney. Lambert no doubt came over to England under one or other of the many neighbouring nobles and military commanders, but there is no record that he was either granted or given lands by William the Conqueror in return for his services, though he certainly acquired them in Lincolnshire.

At that time Norton Disney was given to Judith, a niece of the Conqueror, who married Waltheof, Earl of Huntingdon. True to her name she is said to have betrayed her lord's secret plan to murder the king, 'she being inclined to a second husband'. In the year 1073 Waltheof was arrested and beheaded at midnight outside the walls of Winchester. Judith's descendants continued to hold the lordship for some 150 years until the abeyance of the barony.

Though the Disney connection with the parish is certainly of a very early date, there is a complete blank in their records until about the time of King John. There is strong evidence, however, that they settled here very shortly after the Conquest as sub-vassals of the baronial house of Huntingdon. There were certainly at least five feudal lordships held by the Disneys between 1066 and 1461 when the fifth and last of them was killed in the Wars of the Roses at Towton Field, though whether as a Yorkist or Lancastrian is not known. William, whose effigy, together with that of his wife and daughter, is in the church was one of these five lords, and probably the third by the date of the tomb.

Their real acquisition of wealth came with the general scramble which ensued throughout England after the Dissolution of the Monasteries by Henry VIII in 1536. William Disney, the principal figure in the palimpsest brass was, in 1532, Sheriff of Lincolnshire. Four years later both he and his brother John possessed, by whatever unrecorded means, large estates in that county.

William obtained the valuable manor of Swinderby, former property of the Knights Hospitallers, together with the hamlet of Morton annexed. John gained the manor of Carlton-le-Moorland, formerly belonging to the Abbey of Thornton. Here he founded the cadet line from which, it is reasonably feasible, Walt Disney descended.

Ten years before this, however, there had been a massive Lincolnshire protest against the proposed Dissolution of the Monasteries, and some 20,000 rebels were very loud in their angry protests. Since the church brass states that both William Disney and his son Richard 'were trewe and faithful to their Prince and country', it is possible the reference was to their services in suppressing these rebels.

Early in the next century a branch of the family moved to Carlton-le-Moorland, the next parish, where the church registers record the burial, in 1615, of Ursula Disney. After her death her husband Thomas removed to Somerton Castle, three miles to the east, the lease of which he had bought. As there was no issue of the marriage, he later sold it to Sir Edward Hussey.

Richard, son of William, both of whom are depicted on the

monumental brass, married twice, firstly a granddaughter of John, Lord Hussey, who had been beheaded in 1537, and secondly Jane, daughter of Sir William Ayscough. She had been previously married to George St Pol, by whom she had a son.

Her youngest sister was Anne Askew, the corrupted spelling of the true name Ayscough, who was born in 1521 at Stalling-borough, in Lincolnshire, three miles from the river Humber, in the church of which are many splendid Ayscough monuments. Her cruel death for her simple faith gave her a tragic part not only in the Disney but in English history.

When quite young she was forced by her father into a marriage with Thomas Kyme, of that very ancient family. After she had borne him two children he drove her out because he found her religious principles were obnoxious to him. She made her way to London, apparently to seek a divorce, and was kindly received by Katherine Parr. Her husband had meanwhile lodged the very serious charge of heresy against her, which resulted in her being arrested and subjected to such rigorous questioning that she became very ill. Still she remained adamant in her refusal to subscribe to the unreformed doctrine of the real presence in the sacrament and was imprisoned. As under constant questioning and examination she still persisted in her refusal to accept the charge of heresy, she was sent to the Tower and put on the dreadful rack. Sir Richard Rich and Chancellor Wriothesley themselves turned the screws. Even under this cruel torture she did not yield, but she was left permanently maimed. As if this were not enough she was sentenced to death at the stake as a heretic.

So crippled was she by the tortures she had to be carried to Smithfield in a chair, and her body tied to the stake by a chain. Still refusing to alter her beliefs she died with three other martyrs on 16 July 1546. She was only twenty-five.

By his first marriage Richard had seven sons and five daughters. He was succeeded, curiously enough, by his youngest son Daniel, who married Mary Molyneux. By her he had three daughters, one of whom, Elizabeth, married William, son of Sir William Staunton, and two sons, Henry, who succeeded him, and Francis. It was Daniel, Sheriff of Lincolnshire in 1582, who put up the great family brass in the church, and his will, proved in 1587, is a most interesting and revealing document of a wealthy country gentleman of those times.

After desiring to be buried in Norton Disney church he left several bequests. The first of these was 'to my Lord Chief Justice of England my pyed colte lately taken into my stable for a memory of his Lordship's goodwill toward me at all tymes'. To his wife he left 'my velvet gown and one third of my household stuff . . . a white silver salt, a silver bowl parcel gilt that I bought at Kingerby . . . my coche with two baye geldings that were accustomed to draw the same. . . . My wife shall remayne and be in the house with my son Henry Disney at Norton, so long as the same agree together, or els she to goe to Kingerby quietlie'. Daniel must have been a great lover of falconry for there are numerous bequests of 'my best hawk' and 'my best tercels' and 'my newest falcon' to various members of his family.

An even more interesting document connected with him is the rhyming pedigree drawn up by Sir William Staunton when his son married Daniel's daughter Elizabeth.

> This Wilyam married Elizabeth
> (God graunt them still acorde)
> Daughter to Daniel Disney, 'Squire,
> Of Norton Disney Lorde
>
> An house of great antiquitie,
> As many that I can name,
> And when she a mayden was
> All did commend her fame.

It goes on at some length, enumerating her various skills and calling for a heavenly blessing and a speedy issue.

Daniel Disney was succeeded by his son Henry, who though living and dying at Norton Disney, in all probability founded the line of Swinderby and The Hyde, the latter being the manor near Ingatestone, Essex, held by him. He claimed to be twentieth in direct descent from Lambert Disney the head of the line.

47

Henry married twice, having a son and daughter by his first wife and two sons by his second. He was succeeded by his eldest son William, who died in 1656 and was succeeded in turn by his eldest son Molyneux, the last of that name, who succeeded to the entailed estate and made a complicated claim to the Barony of Hussey.

He fought with Cromwell in the Civil Wars in which Lincolnshire was heavily involved, but like many others considered it expedient to go over to Charles II at the Restoration. In 1674 he sold the manor to the Duke of Albemarle. By his marriage with the daughter of Sir Robert Mounson he had thirteen children, seven daughters and six sons. Only one of the sons lived to manhood, and then, like Monmouth himself, was beheaded for his part in that ill-fated rising. With his death the senior male line terminated.

The cadet line of Disney of Swinderby and The Hyde, near Ingatestone in Essex had the same arms and crest as the senior line. The extant American line of which Walt Disney was a collateral descendant thus continues this very ancient Norman family for just over 900 years of history.

DYMOKE

Arms: Sable, two lions passant in pale argent ducally crowned or.

The dramatic title of Champion of England, so splendidly chivalric, has been proudly borne by the Dymoke family from the coronation of Richard II in 1377 until that of Queen Elizabeth II in 1953. For almost 600 years of history they have fulfilled the office first granted by William the Conqueror to Robert Marmion, whose ancestors had been hereditary Champions to the Dukes of Normandy, and inherited by Sir John Dymoke when he married the great-granddaughter of Philip Marmion, the last feudal baron of that family.

The specified duty of the Champion was 'to ride completely armed upon a barbed horse into Westminster Hall after the coronation and there to challenge to combat with whomsoever should deny the king's right to the crown'. The feudal grandeur, colour, and splendour of this ceremony represented English traditional pageantry at its very best, and continued through the coronations of every sovereign until that of George IV.

After the procession to Westminster Hall from the Abbey,

where the crowning took place, the king sat down amongst the nobility of his land to a great banquet. Following the giving and receiving of many rich and traditional gifts from various peers, and the removal of the first course from the laden tables, the huge hall, beneath its double hammer beam roof, suddenly resounded to a fanfare of trumpets from the royal trumpeters in their gallery above the entrance.

The gates were flung open and there beneath the Gothic archway the Champion of England came riding into the great hall on a richly caparisoned piebald horse. He was completely clad in shining steel armour, a great panache of plumes upon his helm, and carrying a gauntlet in his right hand. On his right and left rode his two squires in half armour, and on their right and left walked two pages, the former carrying the Champion's lance, the latter bearing his targe, or shield, upon which were emblazoned the Dymoke arms. The Champion was preceded by two trumpeters, one of whom was a sergeant trumpeter bearing a mace, two sergeants of arms also bearing maces, and a herald.

The trumpeters blew three loud blasts and the Champion, in clear ringing tones, issued his traditional challenge:

> If any person of what degree soever, high or low, shall deny or gainsay our Sovereign Lord King, the last being deceased, to be right heir to the Imperial Crown of this kingdom or that he ought not to enjoy the same, here is his Champion who saith that he lieth and is a false traitor, being ready in person to combat with him and in this quarrel will adventure his life against him on whatsoever day shall be appointed.

After pausing a few moments the Champion, to support the challenge, threw his gauntlet clattering on the ground. Amidst shouts of 'Long live the King' from the whole assembly, the herald picked up the gauntlet and returned it to the Champion, who with his cavalcade, moved half way into the hall and repeated the ceremony. The third time he rode to the foot of the throne, the herald read the challenge at the top of the steps, and the Champion flung his gauntlet down defiantly for the last time. No acceptance of the challenge has ever been recorded.

The Royal Cup-bearer then handed the king a gold cup full of wine from which he drank to his Champion and passed the cup to him. The Champion, after himself drinking and crying out 'Long live His Majesty', handed the cup to one of his pages to bear away for him as his traditional perquisite of office. The number of gold cups which the Dymoke family have collected through the centuries must be of inestimable value, both personal and material.

In earlier times they could be seen at the family home of Scrivelsby Court in the hamlet of Scrivelsby, four miles from the Lincolnshire market town of Horncastle. It was badly burned in the eighteenth century, restored, and recently demolished, the present Champion living in the converted sixteenth century gate house.

Some three or four hundred yards away is the church, filled with family monuments, tombs, and brasses. Here are the monuments of Lewis Dymoke, perhaps the most splendid, Champion to the first two Hanoverian kings, George I and II; to John, Champion to George III; and Sir Robert, Champion to Richard III, Henry VII, and Henry VIII. Sir Robert built the well-known sixteenth-century Lion Gate, entrance to the deer park, standing on the side of the Horncastle to Revesby road which passes through Scrivelsby. There is also a large effigy of a knight in chain armour said to be that of the last great feudal baron Philip Marmion, who died in 1292, leaving four daughters and no male issue, so that the barony fell into abeyance.

In 1350 his great-granddaughter Margaret de Ludlow, sole heiress of the manor of Scrivelsby, married Sir John Dymoke, bringing to him not only the ancient baronial Lincolnshire estate but also the hereditary title of Champion of England. His right to this was immediately challenged by a kinsman but was over-ruled by the Court of Claims, thus enabling Sir John to perform the ceremony of Champion for the first time at the coronation of Richard II in 1377. After the death of Sir John his wife remained a widow, and their son Thomas was over sixty years of age when his mother died, having acted for her as Champion to Henry IV and Henry V. His son, Sir Philip, became Champion to Henry VI, who issued a mandate to the Keeper of the Royal Wardrobe 'to deliver to his Champion such furniture as his ancestors had been accustomed to have on such occasions'. This included an elaborate suit of armour, a richly caparisoned horse, and twenty yards of crimson satin.

The peaceful existence of the Dymokes, however, was soon to come to an end, as with so many other families during the blood bath of the Wars of the Roses. It came with the marriage of Sir Philip's son, Sir Thomas, to Margaret, daughter of Lionel, sixth Lord Welles. In the year 1469 Richard Nevill, Earl of Warwick, 'the Kingmaker', made a bid to restore Henry VI to the throne and depose the Yorkist Edward IV. Sir Thomas Dymoke, who was Champion at the latter's coronation, and his brother-in-law Richard, Lord Willoughby and Welles, at once joined the Lancastrian cause. Warwick appointed Sir Robert, the latter's son, as commander of the forces.

When Edward IV heard of this treachery he summoned both Dymoke and Willoughby to Westminster, but fearing the king's anger they sought sanctuary there instead of attending his court. In return for his promise of safety, however, they came out of sanctuary and the king demanded that Lord Willoughby's son should lay down his arms. This promise his father gave, sending a messenger at once with the royal decision and command. Then the king, together with Lord Willoughby and Sir Thomas Dymoke, set out at the head of his army for Stamford.

Sir Robert Welles, who had received his father's letter before the arrival of the king, adamantly refused to lay down his arms. Edward IV, in an outburst of savage temper, ordered the immediate execution of Lord Willoughby and Sir Thomas Dymoke and they were both beheaded. Sir Robert, in revenge, launched a furious but hasty and ill-advised attack against the king's forces, was defeated, taken prisoner, and also beheaded.

Though all three were attainted and stripped of their honours and titles the king did restore to Sir Thomas Dymoke's son, Sir Robert, all his father's forfeited honours, including the hereditary title of Champion. Once again, as so often happened in those perilously uncertain times, a family near to ruin, dishonour, and even extinction, had the good fortune to survive.

This Sir Robert, who lies in Scrivelsby church, and who built the Lion Gate, was Champion to no less than three sovereigns, Richard III, Henry VII, and Henry VIII. He not only kept his head intact during the reign of the last monarch, but fought with distinction under him in the French wars at Tournai and was there appointed King's Treasurer. He died in 1546 and was succeeded by his son Sir Edward who was also three times Champion: to Edward VI, Queen Mary, and Queen Elizabeth. He married Anne, sister and co-heiress of Gilbert, Lord Talboys of Kyme, whose portrait hangs in the College of Arms, London.

Sir Robert, the son of this marriage, was a devoted Catholic and suffered badly under Elizabeth's persecution of them. In spite of being in a very weak state of health he was dragged before the Bishop of Lincoln for examination, was imprisoned in that city for his heresy, and died there.

In 1641 Charles Dymoke, Champion to Charles I, was a staunch Royalist. He died at Oxford in 1644 and was buried at Scrivelsby, leaving £2,000 to the Royal cause. For this single act of generosity the Parliamentarians fined his successor £7,000. This vast sum of money brought the family to the verge of ruin, and it was very many years before they recovered. His cousin Edward, who succeeded, was Champion to Charles II and was knighted by that monarch as some compensation 'for his loyalty and great suffering both in person and estate'.

Of Edward's grandson, Charles, who was Champion to William and Mary, and Queen Anne, it is recorded 'he held certain lands by exhibiting to the people on a certain day annually a milk white bull with black ears to be run down by them, cut into pieces, and given among the poor'. He was succeeded by his brother Lewis, Champion to George I and George II, who died at the age of ninety-one and whose splendid memorial tablet is in Scrivelsby church.

John, the son of Lewis Dymoke's cousin, Edward, was Cham-

pion at the coronation of George III. His younger son, another
John, was rector of Scrivelsby and Prebendary of Lincoln, and as
he 'deemed the office to be incompatible with the office of a
clergyman' he appointed his son Henry, created the first baronet,
as his deputy at the coronation of George IV.

This ceremony, the last one the Champion carried out in all its
traditional form of rich medieval pageantry, was quite probably
the most splendid of all, if the full report of an eye-witness, published in the *Gentleman's Magazine* of that time is to be believed.
The Champion on this occasion was escorted by two of the fore-
most figures of that time, on his right by the Duke of Wellington,
and on his left by Lord Howard of Effingham, both magnificently
dressed in crimson and ermine robes, wearing their coronets, and
carrying their staves of office. 'A Mahomedan Paradise' wrote
this eye-witness of the huge assembly of peeresses in their robes
and coronets. The Privy Councillors wore clothes of white and
blue satin, with trunk hose as in the time of Queen Elizabeth I.
The pages wore coats of scarlet with gold lace, white silk hose, and
white rosettes.

Immediately after the Champion had ridden his cavalcade from
the ceremony, his page bearing the traditional gold cup, Garter
King of Arms, surrounded by all his officers, read the Proclama-
tion from the steps of the throne in Latin, French, and English,
repeating it three times in the reverse order of the Champion's
entry. At the entrance all the heralds cried out 'Largesse', a
medieval privilege at tournaments when it was their custom to ask
for gifts of money for their services.

The high privilege of this ancient chivalric office gives the
Champion the right to quarter his own personal arms with that
of his office, a silver sword on a black shield, as it seems certain
the feudal Marmions did before them, their personal arms being
Vairee, a fess gules. The Dymoke motto *Pro Rege dimico*, 'I fight for
the king', is a clever pun on their name, as was their former crest
of two donkeys or 'mokes', now changed into hares by dis-
approving members of the family.

The office of Champion is still an important one, even if much of the rich medieval colour and splendour of pageantry has disappeared. At the coronations of Edward VII and George V a Dymoke, as a precedence, bore the Standard of England into Westminster Abbey. At the coronation of George VI the Champion bore the Union standard, as he did also at the coronation of the present Queen Elizabeth II in 1953, thus continuing through almost six centuries a hereditary and unique title which the Dymoke family have always so justly and so proudly borne.

FETTIPLACE

Arms: Gules, two chevrons argent.

Every year hundreds of English and many American tourists visit the beautiful church of St Mary, Swinbrook, near Burford in Oxfordshire, to see some of the most remarkable stone effigies in the world. These are the tomb monuments to the Fettiplace family, one of the most prolific and ubiquitous of English county families, whose male line continued from the Conquest to the reign of George III.

The monuments by William Byrd fill the whole north side of the chancel and dominate the church. The six life-size figures recline on their marble slabs, like passengers lying in cabin bunks of ships. Three of them are in full armour, posed with their heads on their hands, their legs straight and together, as if they are sleeping, with neatly trimmed beards and faces of expressive elegance and aristocracy; and three are leaning curiously forward upon the right elbow, their left legs bent up and towards them as if in pain, alert and gazing out beyond their niches into some future only they can see.

All of them had once lived in that splendid and beautiful manor house of Swinbrook, close to the church, of which no single stone remains today, and only the faintest traces may be seen to outline vaguely the shape of all its former foundations. This, and the fifteenth-century manor houses of Childrey and East Shefford in Berkshire, were in constant occupation by the family, and now only a part of Childrey is left, and, though much restored, retains even today sufficient evidence of its former architectural beauty.

The Swinbrook manor house had been created with all the skill, taste, and wisdom of a family which owned three of the most beautiful examples of this type of Tudor architecture in England. It stood on gently rising ground above the lovely little river Windrush, winding its way through the green meadows. Anthony Fettiplace purchased it in 1503. He then began to rebuild it to resemble the original manor house of East Shefford. Indeed, according to writers of the time, it even excelled in splendour and beauty the moated manor house in Berkshire where, in a vast and picturesque banqueting hall, were displayed with pride on the windows, and on the corbels supporting the great oak roof, the five blue shields of the royal house of Portugal. Swinbrook also had a magnificent hall, the great and lofty windows of which were filled with the painted shields in stained glass of all their many alliances.

The earliest evidence of the now familiar family arms of *gules, two chevrons argent*, is to be seen in the cloisters of Canterbury Cathedral. They are displayed on the bosses of the intersections of the rib-mouldings on the ground vaulting of the bays. The Fettiplace shield forms one of those bosses and is in the fourth compartment of the north pane of the cloisters.

The name Fettiplace has had various spellings, the first of which was Geoffrey Petitpas on a document in the reign of King John. In Norman times it was probably 'petitplace'. In America it has become Pheteplace, Phetteplace, Fetteplace or Phetiplace.

Although the first Fettiplace came over with William the Conqueror as his Gentleman Usher, nothing is known of this family until 1232 when Adam, the head of the future line, was imprisoned in Oxford 'for wounding and beating the Clerks of

Oxford Schools'. Adam was an extremely wealthy merchant or tradesman, and owned considerable lands in Oxfordshire and Berkshire. He was later twice elected mayor, and finally chief magistrate, of the very city that had imprisoned him. Only twenty years later Walter Fettiplace, probably his son, was heavily fined by a jury for ejection of certain of his tenants because of rent arrears, and 'for beating and ill-using the lady of the house'.

This behaviour was in complete contrast to the general pattern of conduct the Fettiplace family followed for the next 500 years, when they seemed to have achieved nothing but vast fortunes, distinguished and wealthy alliances with even richer families and the acquisition of so much property that a couplet was soon circulating around England:

> 'The Lacies, the Tracies, and the Fettiplaces
> Own all the manors, the parks and the chases'.

In fact they owned no less than forty-seven manor houses in Oxfordshire and Berkshire, houses in London, countless acres of parks, woodlands and farms in both the former counties as well as Essex and Gloucestershire. There were ten heads of the family in various lines of male descent in these several counties, with some of the most complicated pedigrees to be found in the whole of English genealogy.

Perhaps the most interesting event in their history, however, was the emigration of at least one if not more of the family to America, probably from Essex via London and Bristol or Southhampton. Their links with American history became of the highest importance. A certain Henry Clitherow had two daughters. One married Dr Thomas Fettiplace the elder, the other married Dr Thomas Fettiplace the younger. The Clitherow family owned property in Essex known as Joyces and Highams Manor. This property came to a David Williams, who left the income from it to 'The College of New England' as it was known in the 1600s, now Harvard University. The income is collected and paid even today.

There is no doubt at all, therefore, that one or more of the

Fettiplaces who went to America had done so in the very considerable emigration of Puritans from Essex, which had become the centre of this new challenge to orthodox church teaching. Such men as Cotton, Hooker, Winthrop, Williams, even Cromwell himself, lent their protection to the movement. One of the most fanatical of them, as is evident from his extant writings, was Dr Thomas Fettiplace the elder, who had married into the Clitherow family.

The principal centre in Essex of all these activities was a place called Otes. Here lived a certain Sir William Masham who willingly opened his house for meetings. His chaplain was the famous Roger Williams who later founded Rhode Island, one of the six New England States. He first settled there in 1636 when he and others, as a separatist group of Congregationalists expelled from Massachusetts by the Puritans, set up on their own.

Another rabid Puritan in Essex was John Winthrop, who later became Governor of the colony of Massachusetts, 1629–34 and 1637–49. He sailed in the *Arabella* from Yarmouth with 900 colonists in 1630, and helped to found Boston. With him went his great friend Josselin who visited him several times in his frequent voyages between America and Essex.

From this time forward the name of Phetteplace becomes very much in evidence in America, especially in the various Rhode Island records, and is clearly the reason why so many Americans come to visit the church at Swinbrook before extending their researches on this oddly ubiquitous family. In 1782 a ship set sail for Newburyport, Massachusetts, called the *Antelope*, of about 100 tons and bearing a letter of marque. It was owned by Tristram and Dalton of Newburyport and commanded by Captain Edward Fettyplace.

Other important members of the American side of the family were Richard and William Phetteplace, who accompanied Captain John Smith of Pocahontas fame, to Virginia in 1607. A Philip Phetteplace lived at Portsmouth, Rhode Island, where, before his death in July 1681, he witnessed the will of another colonist, Phillip Sherman, who came from Dedham in Essex, England.

This Philip Phetteplace was admitted as a freeman to Portsmouth, Rhode Island on 22 September 1671.

A Walter Phetteplace who claimed to be a direct descendant of the first Fettiplace who came over with the Conqueror, was appointed by Governor Jencks as Assistant Deputy to the General Assembly when Glocester was set off from Providence in 1731. In 1746 he urged the authorities to keep sufficient money in the General Treasury for use against any hostile power seeking to attack the colony. He died in Providence in 1753.

At the beginning of the fifteenth century an event took place in the Fettiplace family that not only added very considerably to its wealth and importance, but brought into it a strange romance. This was the marriage of Sir Thomas Fettiplace, owner of the manors of East Shefford and Childrey, with Beatrice, widow of Gilbert Talbot, Baron of Ircherfield and Blackmere. This lady was a daughter of the royal house of Portugal, and the well-favoured, handsome, wealthy Sir Thomas pursued his prey with all the determination and resolution so evident in the sculptured features of his effigy in East Shefford church. Lady Beatrice was Lord Talbot's second wife, his first being Joan Plantagenet, granddaughter of Edward III.

'The family,' wrote Bishop White Kennett, 'received a great addition of blood and honour by marrying Beatrix, daughter of the King of Portugal, which match is mentioned and allowed of in the pedigree of the Kings of Portugal.' Yet confusion was rife as to the Lady Beatrice's exact lineage, and there was found in the correspondence of one of the rectors of East Shefford, the following letter, which does very little to illuminate the darkness of conjecture. It was written from the Legation of Portugal, and dated 20 August 1887:

Sir, Pray accept my best thanks for your letter relating to the Fettiplace Tomb. All that I can say in reply to it is that in 1405 an illegitimate daughter of King John I of Portugal, named Beatrice, married Thomas, Earl of Arundel and Surrey. Left a widow she re-married, in 1415, to Gilbert Talbot, Baron of Ircherfield and Blackmere, K.G. She was again left a widow in 1419. I am convinced that she did not marry Sir Thomas Fettiplace as her third husband. I am sorry that I am unable to give you further information.

(Signed M. D'Antas)

Whether this statement was right or wrong, the Lady Beatrice died on Christmas Day 1447, and she and 'her dear lord' lie buried under a beautiful alabaster altar-tomb in the long disused church of East Shefford, standing in forlorn beauty by the winding river Lambourn. This was once the private chapel of the Fettiplace family, and it was fitting that this lady of royal blood, with her slight figure, her mantle of state and mitred head-dress being witnesses to her dignity, should lie here. On another canopied tomb of Purbeck marble, opposite, are brass effigies of their great-grandson John and his wife Dorothy.

Sir Thomas left three sons. His first, William, had an only daughter who married into the Unton family, and in the Unton Chapel in Faringdon church the Fettiplace arms are most prolific. James, the second son, settled at Maidencote, his line ending in a daughter who married Edmund Dunch of Little Wittenham. The son of this marriage married Mary, daughter of Sir Henry Cromwell, an aunt of the Protector, Oliver Cromwell. John, the third, was a citizen and draper of London, and of the household of King Henry VI; for it was fashionable at that time for the nobility and gentry, and even royalty, to become members of one of the great city guilds. It may well be that his position at court was largely influenced by his mother's royal blood, and his knowledge of Portuguese was undoubtedly advantageous when King Henry presented to the King of Portugal 'a certain gilt garter, ornamented with pearls and flowers', for which he received in return forty pounds, which the king commanded to be paid to John 'for his costs and expenses'.

John Fettiplace grew exceedingly rich and amassed much wealth during his residence in London, due in no small measure to his marriage with Joan Fabian, widow of John Horne, Alderman of London. He died in 1461, leaving the great manor of East Shefford to his son Richard.

This Richard married into the Besils family of Besils Leigh; his second son, Anthony, resided first at Swinbrook in Oxfordshire and then at Childrey, where he became sheriff of the county. He married the sister of Sir Adrian Fortescue, who after long being in favour with Henry VIII, was beheaded on Tower Hill for alleged conspiracy. The third son, Sir Thomas, lived in the beautiful manor house of Compton Beauchamp. He lies buried in Abingdon church. William, the youngest son, though as rich as his brothers was disinclined to mix in court circles or public affairs. He lived quietly at Letcombe, and spent the whole of his life attending to his estates and tenants, and rebuilding the tower of Childrey church.

At his death he bequeathed vast lands to the Provost and Scholars of The Queen's College, Oxford, on condition they kept in constant repair the aisle where he lay buried, and the alms-houses and schools he had founded. As that most learned and indefatigable Fettiplace authority, J. R. Dunlop, once wrote: 'It is more than likely that it is owing to his foresight in vesting these powers in an Oxford college that so many interesting traces of his family remain in Childrey church, and the charities he created still exist.'

By virtue of their high standing in the two counties of Berkshire and Oxfordshire, they automatically became commissioners, sheriffs, and knights of the shires. Sir Thomas, who owned the manor house of Compton Beauchamp, was appointed, in 1520, to accompany Henry VIII to the Field of Cloth of Gold. An Edward, of Chively and Donnington Castle in Berkshire, was appointed, in 1539, to receive Anne of Cleves on her arrival in England from Düsseldorf. A John, probably of the Fernham and cadet line, was a colonel in the Parliamentarian Army, and Governor of Cirencester, which town he loyally garrisoned for Cromwell. Another John, who was a great Royalist, was, when the Articles of Surrender were agreed to, fined the huge sum in those days of £1,943; for this great family, like so many others, was split apart in the bloody civil war.

One Fettiplace wrote a play called *Injured Innocence*, which was produced at Drury Lane. A Thomas Fettiplace, of St Martin-in-the-Fields, was killed by a fall from a horse; his brother John, in 1665, 'dyed of the sicknesse and was buryed abroad'. There was a certain Thomas who bequeathed 'ten pounds to help my nephew out of prison'; and a George who disinherited his son and left him only 7s 6d a week and his sword and guns. A John left 'alle my whyte swannes upon Thamyse' to his eldest son. Another George, who, when Master of the Bench, died of the plague in 1577, was buried at Coln St Aldwyn, Gloucestershire. He was described in a history of Pembrokeshire as 'that worthy and learned Gentleman, Mr. George Phetiplace, who contynued Justice till untymely death bereafte us of him'.

A Sir John Fettiplace 'died verie suddenly, not without foul suspi'tion of his being poyson'd by his wife Susanna. Shee was examined by certaine Justices of the Peace, but nothing could be made cleare against her. Afterwards having 200l per annum settled by the Feteplaces on her shee retired to Lechlade, and took to her third husband, a brisk, gay, and handsome young man, Sir Thomas Cutler, for of Sir John she was weary, he being a dul fellow.'

There is said to be a Fettiplace ghost, seen in recent years as an armed man kneeling at the altar of Swinbrook church. Was this perhaps the restless and unhappy Sir John praying for the soul of Susanna who poisoned him, or for 'the brisk young fellow' she later married?

When Henry VIII, in the year 1539, dissolved the great monasteries of England and all monastic buildings, which for centuries had been the quiet and ordered homes of so many monks and nuns, great numbers of vowesses were turned out homeless into a very unsheltered world; and among them were Eleanor, Ursula, and Elizabeth Fettiplace who, during their lifetime, had taken shelter in Syon in Middlesex, and Ambresbury Priory in Wiltshire. They were granted pitiful pensions, in one case only £6 a year.

Edmund Fettiplace was created a Knight of the Royal Oak by King Charles II, who conferred this specially created honour on his followers as a reward for their services both to himself and his father. Sir Edmund was Sheriff of Oxfordshire in 1675, and in 1686 was granted special permission to enclose land for a park at Swinbrook. He it was who, in that same year, commissioned William Byrd to erect the unique monuments in Swinbrook church to honour and commemorate his father, his uncle and himself.

Sir Edmund and his three brothers in turn inherited the baronetcy, and all four were unmarried; so the light of danger was already showing to threaten the continuance of the family line, for as each one died there was less and less possibility of an heir. This is indeed strange when one remembers those early and even desperate attempts by nearly all the various ancestors to perpetuate their line by obits, masses, charities, and sums of money. It is almost incomprehensible in the case of Sir Charles, who not only kept a mistress named Miss Ferguson, but actually had an illegitimate child by her named Arabella. Instead of marrying his mistress he offered John Secker the sum of £1,000 if he would marry Arabella. Secker indignantly refused and Arabella was summarily married to Thomas Stevens, and went to live in Banbury. It is not known if the same sum of money was involved. Sir Charles and Sir Lorenzo were each in turn sheriffs of Oxfordshire.

Sir George, last of the four brothers and last male heir of the line, is represented in Swinbrook church by a most beautiful alabaster bust carved by John Annis of London, this being one of his finest works. His face is open, pleasant, kind, humorous, giving no indication at all of the vicious round of pleasure he led from start to finish of his life. It is a little disturbing, therefore, when reading the eulogistic and flattering inscription on this monument, to remember just how he lived and died. His life, apart from very generous and quite considerable charities and bequests, the largest of which was the bequest of £1,000 to the Governors of Christ's Hospital to be held in trust for the education of two poor children from Swinbrook, was spent in one illicit love affair after another.

He loved racing, cock fighting, cards, women, wine, and all to excess. Even in an age when, without such things, no man could consider himself a gentleman, he exceeded the undefined limits; but short of actually marrying and producing an heir Sir George did everything else in his power to perpetuate a name he himself knew only too well would die out at his death. It is quite inexplicable why, with such a strong desire to do this, he did not even try to marry and beget a son and heir from one of his several mistresses.

On 7 April 1743, Sir George returned to the Bull Hotel at, Burford in Oxfordshire, after a day at the races. The actual reason for his death is not quite certain. He had been drinking heavily, as was his custom, and was probably engaged in the settlement of some heavy wager, made either during or after the races. He suddenly became involved in a quarrel, during which he had a stroke from which he never recovered.

Sir George died as he had lived all through that rich and bucolic age, surrounded by his drunken cronies, guineas, empty bottles and glasses, lace ruffles, swords and cocked hats, in an atmosphere of tobacco smoke, ribald wit, and blasphemy. It was an ignominious end to a family whose motto through the centuries was 'Fortune and Grace'. If there was no outstanding example of the latter there was plenty of evidence of the former. It is ironic, too, that a line which started with the imprisonment of the first should end with the death of the last male heir in a tavern.

All that is left of this most prolific and ubiquitous family are its charities, of which one is a gift of green coats to the poor of Swinbrook, that being the livery colour of the family, a communion cup in constant use at the same church and bearing the engraved family arms, and scattered through several English counties their well-known coat of arms, *gules, two chevrons argent.*

FITZWARINE

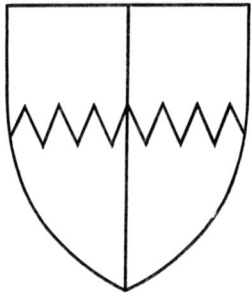

Arms: Quarterly argent and gules, per fess indented.

The splendid parish church of Wantage, in Berkshire, which the
FitzWarine family first built in the thirteenth century and then
maintained wholly or in part for over 400 years, has abundant
evidence of their existence.

On the north side of the chancel is the dilapidated but still
beautiful alabaster altar tomb of Sir William FitzWarine (or
Fitzwaryn), known as Le Frere, and created the twenty-sixth
Garter Knight in 1361. His impressive figure in its Garter robe
lies beside his wife Amicia, at prayer and wearing a coif. Such was
his personal wealth that whilst fighting as a banneret in the French
wars he took with him one knight and ten archers on horseback,
all fully armed and equipped.

On a wall not far away and in the main body of the church is
one of the finest monumental brasses to be seen in England. It is
the five foot high effigy of his son, Sir Ivo FitzWarine. He is in
complete armour; his feet, encased in their pointed sollerets with
rowel spurs, rest on a boldly engraved heraldic lion. His head, in
its pointed bascinet, rests on his tournament helm. His sword

hangs straight down on his left side. He has a moustache, which for a short period of monumental brass history was fashionable, and enables accuracy of dating, in this case, 1414. His crest was a swan between ostrich feathers which he wore when serving under Thomas of Woodstock in the reign of Richard II at the siege of Nantes.

The entry of the Norman family of FitzWarine into English history was dramatic and legendary enough, beginning as it did in the tournament lists. Its departure was even more so, since for nearly 600 years it has been associated with the connected story of Dick Whittington and his cat.

The first FitzWarine was committed by William the Conqueror to the defence of the Marches towards Wales. He carried out his military tasks with considerable skill, but he did much more than that to continue his name. There was at this time a lord of Whittington in Shropshire who had two beautiful daughters, one of whom, Mallet, had resolved to marry none but a knight of great prowess. Her father had appointed a meeting of noble young men for a tournament at Peverel's Place on the Peke, from which she was to select the champion. The two most distinguished contestants were the King of Scotland's son, and the Baron of Burgundy; but to the surprise of everyone they were both vanquished by an unknown young man who not only claimed his rich and beautiful prize, but also the lordship and castle of Whittington which went with it. Here he founded the Abbey of Adderbury.

Sir Fulke was the first son born of this marriage. He, as romantic as his father, fell deeply in love with his tutor's daughter Hawise, and married her, proceeding with her father to Ireland and assisting him in his wars against Walter de Lacie. In 1122 he was created by Henry I Steward of the Royal Household, and Governor of the Marches of Wales. It is said that he was once playing chess with Prince John, son of Henry II—who hated losing any game—when they fell out over a move made by one of them. John, who had a most vicious and dangerous temper (he was once found chewing his mattress in almost lunatic rage), suddenly swept all the pieces away, picked up the board and crashed it over Fulke's head. It says much for the courage and standing of Fulke that, without a moment's hesitation, he wrenched the board away from the hands of the prince and retaliated with such vigour that the board broke over the prince's head, the force of the blow being so violent that he almost died. It would have been instant sentence of death for any but Fulke, and Henry evidently pardoned him, knowing and fearing as he did the danger of his son's temper.

This rash action, however, was never forgotten by John, and when he became king he seized the FitzWarine castle of Whittington and conferred it upon one of his favourites. Fulke, son of Sir Fulke, furious at this act of gross injustice, came out in open rebellion with his brothers against the king, and was outlawed. Through the mediation of the king's brother the Earl of Salisbury, and the Bishop of Norwich, the outlawry was reversed and the castle restored upon payment of 200 marks and two coursers. Before very long, however, he was again at war with John and on the side of the barons. For this he was excommunicated by the Pope and his castles and lands once more seized by the crown.

When Henry III came to the throne they were again restored though for an even heavier fine. Fulke fought with distinction against the Welsh under the Earl of Pembroke, but at the battle of Lewes, 1263, he lost his life fighting for the king against Simon de Montfort. He was drowned in a nearby river, his heavy armour weighing him down. He was one of the most celebrated of the feudal lords, brave, headstrong, proud, independent, and as rash as his father had been. Indeed this quality was inherited right through the line.

His son was elevated to the peerage and created the first baron in 1295. In the same year he was granted the very valuable lordship of the manor of Wantage, Berkshire, formerly the Wessex Saxon palace of the kings where Alfred the Great was born. He was also granted the high privilege of holding a market at Cheping-Lambourn. This charter lasted right up to 1874 when the weekly market was held for the last time by two old farmers who used to meet in an inn and transact business to preserve the medieval right. With the death of one of them the charter became extinct.

Fulke was also created a Knight of the Bath. He married the Princess Margaret, daughter of the Prince of Powys-Wenwynwyn. He had considerable trouble with his additional rights to hold a fair at Wantage. His father had made an arrangement with the Abbot of Abingdon to end the abbot's own fair at Shellingford in Oxfordshire, in favour of his own at Wantage, in exchange for certain other concessions.

A serious event took place when Lord FitzWarine was accused of having killed a man at Shellingford, where, in spite of his father's agreement, a fair was held. He not only killed this man but compelled all the other frequenters of the fair to go to Wantage and pay toll for their disobedience. He died in 1314.

His son Fulke, second baron, held the high office of Constable of the royal army sent against the rebel barons under the Earl of Lancaster, and fought with courage and determination. He married twice, his second wife being the daughter of Henry Lord Beaumont, styled Earl of Buchan in right of his wife. He died in 1349. The third baron was never summoned to Parliament, but he fought at Crécy under the Black Prince and married the third daughter of Lord Audley. The fourth, fifth, sixth and seventh barons do not seem to have distinguished themselves in any way, other than by wealthy marriages into the families of Courtenay and Botreaux.

The seventh and last baron died in infancy in 1429, leaving his only sister Elizabeth as heiress. Her only daughter married Sir William Bourchier, and the family of FitzWarine became extinct in the male succession.

When Sir Ivo FitzWarine, whose brass is in the church, died in 1414, he left a daughter named Alice. According to Sir Walter Besant, and Stow in his *Survey of London*, this Alice married Richard Whittington, thrice Lord Mayor of London. The immortal story of Dick Whittington and his cat need not be re-told, but the widely accepted story of Sir Ivo's daughter Alice marrying Dick Whittington is at once a legend and a mystery.

A certain Mr Hugh Fitzwarren who was a rich merchant living in Leadenhall Street in London, was one day visited by a very poor, ill-treated orphan, who asked him for work. He said his name was Richard Whittington. He was given a job as a scullion in the kitchen. Here the boy suffered greatly at the hands of a brutal cook, and only went on with his work because of the kindness of his master's daughter Alice, and because of his beloved cat, which he had bought for one penny to keep down the rats and mice infesting his garret, preventing him from sleeping.

It was, however, his master's custom as a merchant that whenever he sent out a ship with his goods, he let each one of his servants venture something in it that God might give him and his ship a greater blessing. Poor Dick had nothing in the world to give but his cat, and this he generously but sadly did, and the *Union* set sail with it on board. After many months of sailing the ship put in at a port on the Barbary coast, where the king of the country had a great palace which was over-run with rats and mice. He was so astonished and delighted to find a cat that he bought it for ten times the value of the whole freight of the ship.

Dick, meanwhile, made desperate by the continued ill-usage of the cook, and no longer having his beloved cat, tied up his few belongings in a bundle and stole away early one morning. As he reached Holloway and paused to rest, he heard Bow bells ring out, 'Turn again Whittington, Lord Mayor of London'. He returned to his pots and spit-turning until, on an unexpected day, his master returned with the great news. Dick, now a very rich man, asked for the hand of Alice and married her.

There is no authentic evidence of the cat story, though Thomas Keightley traced it through Persian, Danish and Italian folk-lore as far back as the thirteenth century. Stow has recorded in his *Survey of London* the following facts.

Richard Whittington, mercer, four time Mayor of London, founded the church of St. Michael called Paternoster Royal in the city of London, and made many endowments to pray for him and his wife Alice. And for Sir William Whittington, Kt. and Dame Joan his wife, and for Hugh Fitzwarren and Dame Molde his wife the father and mother of the said Richard Whittington and Alice his wife.

He then describes how the body of Richard Whittington was three times exhumed and reburied before 'placing his monument over him again which remaineth and so he rested'.

Yet there is no trace whatsoever in the FitzWarine pedigree of a Hugh, or of any wife named Molde. According to Burke's *Extinct Peerage* Sir Ivo FitzWarine left one daughter and heiress. Her name was Eleanor and she married Sir John Chediock. Richard Whittington was said to have been the son of Sir William Whittington, a Gloucestershire knight.

And so all that is left of this once distinguished family is the fine church in Wantage and the beautiful legend of Dick Whittington and his cat. Whether it be accurate or not does not seem to matter, for countless thousands of people have already believed it to be true.

GRENVILLE

Dukes of Buckingham and Chandos

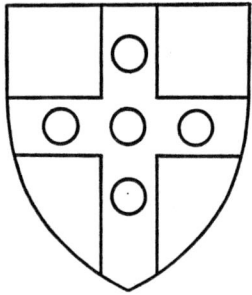

Arms: Vert, on a cross argent five torteaux.

In 1923 the first governors of the newly founded public school at
Stowe, three miles from Buckingham in Buckinghamshire,
bought for £40,000 the huge eighteenth-century palace, for so it
was, upon which its former owners had spent an estimated
£4,000,000 of Victorian money. These were the highly unpopular
Whig grandees, the Temples and Grenvilles, who through inheritance of titles or by marriage, became the last dukes of
Buckingham and Chandos.

Stowe was built in 1697 by Sir Richard Temple, who later
became the first Viscount Cobham. His great-grandmother had
lived to see no less than 700 descendants of the line, which
probably accounts for the 719 painted and named coats of arms to
be seen on the ceiling of the Gothic library built by Sir John Soane.

His sister Hester, who had married Richard Grenville of
Wotton, succeeded him as Viscountess Cobham and was created

72

Countess Temple a month later. Their son George was later Prime Minister of England, and their daughter Hester married William Pitt, another Prime Minister. Thus the great and very unpopular Whig cousinhood was formed.

The second Earl Temple restored Stowe in 1770, only incorporating a little of the original building. From the Earl of Bath's magnificent mansion of Stowe in Cornwall, demolished in 1720, Cobham had bought the chapel wainscoting, part of a Spanish prize of war, and put it in the chapel at Stowe. Robert Adam designed the new south front with portico. The landscape park was laid out successively by Bridgeman, Kent, and 'Capability' Brown. Other features were a Palladian bridge, garden buildings by Kent and Vanbrugh, and a column 115ft high on which was a statue of Lord Cobham as the monarch of all he surveyed, which was very extensive indeed.

About fifteen miles away is the church of Wotton Underwood, where most of the grandees lie buried, each in an enormous vault, preserving in death that fine sense of arrogant grandeur they all of them had in their lifetime.

The Temple who rebuilt Stowe was as unpopular, perhaps even more so, as his brother, the Prime Minister, and hated by the king who spoke of him as 'so disagreeable a fellow there is no bearing him. He is pert, insolent and uncivil'. Walpole called him 'the absolute creature of Pitt and as mischievous as his understanding would let him be'. After Pitt was created Earl Chatham, Temple, whose various ignoble tactics had brought him a formidable number of enemies, resigned and retired to Stowe. Macaulay, whose acidity has probably never been excelled in a description of any other man wrote: 'People track him as they track a mole. It was his nature to grub underground. Wherever a heap of dirt was flung up it might well be suspected that he was at work in some foul crooked labyrinth below'.

Temple did not long enjoy his withdrawal from political life, for one day whilst in one of the ridings of the grounds he was flung out of his pony carriage and fractured his skull. He died in 1779 in his sixty-eighth year. Macaulay's brief unkind epitaph was: 'A man of wealth but no particular talent except intrigue; arrogant and impracticable. His single title to distinction was that he had a large garden with a large piece of water and a great many pavilions and summer houses'.

His nephew George succeeded as third Earl Temple, being created the first Marquess of Buckingham. He married Lady Mary Nugent and assumed the names and arms of Temple and Nugent. His son Richard seems to have had all the arrogance, intolerance, and overbearing manner of the rest of his family. He became MP for Buckingham and Lord Lieutenant of the county, but preferred the life of a rich country gentleman to that of a politician, though always a staunch and dedicated Whig. At the age of twenty he married Lady Anna Eliza Brydges, daughter and heiress of the last Duke of Chandos and so became styled Richard Temple Nugent Brydges Chandos Grenville, assuming the penultimate two names when he was created first Duke of Buckingham and Chandos in 1822 by George IV, the only person that king elevated to the peerage, as well as giving him the coveted Garter. He was also created first Earl Temple of Stowe.

Though his political life was not intense he supported Pitt over the French wars, and was a constant fighter for the abolition of the slave trade, but he, like his father, much preferred to be amongst his many treasures at Stowe. He was finally forced into retirement by violent and painful attacks of gout, a common illness in those days, Pitt, his kinsman, being a martyr to it. He spent money with such prodigality that his avaricious grandfather would have turned in his grave. He began to pile up massive debts in the purchase of various art treasures, and in 1822 entertained the French royal family with such splendid hospitality at Stowe that he became almost bankrupt. He nevertheless had an expensive new yacht built, named the *Anna Eliza* after his wife, embarked at Southampton and sailed abroad for between two and three years before returning to a thirty-day sale of most of his great collection of rare and curious prints, upon which he had lavished a fortune. Such was the value of these prints that dealers came from all over the world to buy them. He died five years later, in 1839, and was buried in the great mausoleum of Wotton.

He was succeeded by his son and only child Richard Plan-tagenet Temple Nugent Brydges Chandos Grenville as third Marquess of Buckingham, second Earl Temple of Stowe, and second Duke of Buckingham and Chandos. He was born at Buckingham House, Pall Mall, the family property in London, and entered Eton as Lord Cobham before going on to Oxford. He was known as Marquess of Chandos and became MP for Buckinghamshire. He was later appointed Lord Privy Seal under Robert Peel. His main political interests were in agriculture and he introduced into parliament the 'Tenant at Will' clause known as the 'Chandos Clause', the only part of the Reform Bill to be identified with anyone's name. Lord Russell said of it 'it destroys the symmetry of the whole measure and frustrates Whig expectations'. He was popularly known as The Farmer's Friend and his constituents at Aylesbury presented him with a signed testimonial of their affection for him.

The duke, however, had far more serious personal problems. On the death of his extravagant father he had inherited a rent-roll of £100,000 a year and massive debts on the estate. He had inherited also his father's extravagant tastes, culture, and jackdaw capacity for collecting. In order to forget the huge clouds of debt over him he wrote a number of historical works of no little value, and the account of his father's yacht voyage. The latter was published after his own death and called *The Private Diary of the Duke of Buckingham and Chandos*. His own peculiarity for spending money was even more eccentric than that of his father, since he had a mania for buying still more land with money he borrowed, the rate of interest paid far exceeding the rents he got in return.

In 1844, when his eldest son came of age, the entail of the estates was cut off, leaving intact the Chandos estates which were entailed on the female heirs. A year later, although she was fully aware of the duke's financial situation, Queen Victoria decided to pay him a visit, staying with her personal retinue for three days. Almost immediately before the intended visit was announced to the duke the bailiffs moved into Stowe. The exasperated and almost bankrupt duke was beside himself. He could not cancel the royal visit nor eject the bailiffs, and after putting his case to them they agreed to wear his livery throughout the royal visit, which they did, apparently giving no suspicion to anyone. The hospitality for the Queen's retinue precipitated the financial crash, for the duke spared nothing in this final splendid gesture, though he managed to avert complete bankruptcy for two more years.

On 31 August 1847, the bailiffs took over again and this time there was no question of wearing livery. All the household effects were distrained, and on 12 September the duke, like his father, left the country, though not in a yacht. He was bankrupt and his total liabilities were over £1,000,000 of Victorian money. The sale lasted forty days; his estates in Oxfordshire, Northamptonshire, and Buckinghamshire fetched £262,990, his household effects surprisingly only £75,562. *The Times* wrote pungently of him. 'A man of the highest rank and of a property not unequal to his rank has thrown away all by folly and extravagance, reducing his honour to the tinsel of a pauper and the baubles of a fool.'

His private life had not been made more happy by his wife, Lady Mary Campbell, daughter of the first Marquess of Breadalbane, whom he had married when he was twenty-two, divorcing him. She continued to live at Stowe, however, and survived him by one year. He lived in London and died in the Great Western Hotel, Paddington Station. His body was taken to Wotton to be buried with all the other members of his family.

He was succeeded by his son, Richard Plantagenet Campbell Grenville, third Earl Temple of Stowe, and third and last Duke of Buckingham and Chandos, who was born in 1823. The full arms borne by the family at this stage were:

Quarterly; 1 and 6 Vert, on a cross argent five torteaux, for Grenville.
 2, Quarterly, 1 and 4 Or, an eagle displayed sable for Leofric;
 2 and 3 Argent, two bars sable each charged with three martlets or for Temple.
 3, Ermine, two bars gules for Nugent.
 4, Argent, on a cross sable a leopard's face or for Brydges.
 5, Or, a pile gules for Chandos.

Like all his predecessors he was MP for Buckinghamshire, but broke right across the family Whig tradition by contesting Oxford as a Conservative, losing to Gladstone. He became chairman of the old London & North Western Railway, and later Governor of Madras, raising for that stricken area a huge famine relief fund. He made almost superhuman efforts to settle his father's debts and clear his bankruptcy, dying of diabetes at Chandos House in London. He had been married twice, having three daughters by his first wife and no issue by the second.

Thus the marquessates of Buckingham and of Chandos, the earldom of Temple of the first creation, and the dukedom of Buckingham and Chandos all became extinct. The earldom of Temple of Stowe, still extant, devolved upon his nephew. It was the end of the great cousinhood, the Whig league of Stowe. By his victory over the last duke at Oxford Gladstone had put the Liberals on the map. Whigs, as a political party, had ceased to exist.

The dukes lie side by side in their huge tombs in the Grenville Chantry Chapel of the church at Wotton Underwood. Above and around them are some 200 or more coloured armorial shields in the windows. Perhaps at the last they found the harmony and peace they had never enjoyed as a family through the 200 years of their eventful Stowe dynasty.

HERBERT

Earls of Pembroke and Montgomery

Arms: Per pale azure and gules, three lions rampant argent.

Wilton House, 2¼ miles west of Salisbury in Wiltshire, has been called the most beautiful house in England. The great south front is certainly one of the glories of English Renaissance architecture. The Grotto, the Palladian bridge over the Nadder, and the Gothic cloister are as well known to the 70,000-odd annual visitors as the famous cedars of Lebanon in the gardens.

The house is filled with priceless treasures, a unique collection of Van Dyck pictures, exquisite ceilings and doors, books, furniture, and busts. The masterpiece, however, is the famous Double Cube room of Inigo Jones and his adopted son Webb, so much coveted by George IV that he offered the fourth Earl of Pembroke as many golden sovereigns as would cover the floor, an area of some 200 square feet. James I, Charles I and Charles II all loved the house. The present Queen has been a guest there, also General Eisenhower and Sir Winston Churchill, the last with such enthusiastic frequency that his sojourns there were known as Winstontides. Shakespeare was said to have performed *As You Like It* and *Twelfth Night* there, and Massinger, Sir Philip Sidney and Ben Jonson were frequent guests.

The Herberts, Earls of Pembroke, have lived in their beautiful house for four centuries, ever since they were granted Wilton by Henry VIII at the dissolution of the monasteries. They claim their descent from Henry Thesaurus, a natural son of Hubertus Camerarius, chamberlain to William Rufus. Thus the Herberts always claim close connection with the crown. In addition they held considerable lands in Wales and were closely linked to the Welsh through marriage alliances.

William Herbert, first Earl of Pembroke, was the natural son of Richard, Gentleman Usher to Henry VIII, and Constable and Porter of Abergavenny Castle. At the age of twenty-five William, when drunk, made a dramatic entry into history by killing a tailor named Vaughan on Bristol Bridge. He escaped through the back streets, fled to France, and enlisted in the French army. 'A mad fighting young fellow,' John Aubrey tells us, 'he was called Black Will Herbert'. His courage, military skill and wit endeared him to both the French king and Henry VIII, and though he could neither read nor write he had a prodigious memory. One of his richest prizes was the grant to him of Nunnery Abbey at Wilton, upon the site of which he built Wilton House.

He moved even closer to the king when he married the sister of Queen Catherine Parr, Henry VIII's last wife. He managed to keep his head from the block and moved smoothly into Edward VI's reign, receiving even greater honours and being created Earl of Pembroke. To celebrate the last he entertained the king and no less than 4,000 of his retinue at Wilton House.

When the Lord Protector Somerset was beheaded for treason he received all his estates and joined the Duke of Northumberland in his abortive attempt to by-pass the Tudor line and put his own son and Lady Jane Grey on the throne. With uncanny intuition Pembroke went over to Mary when she raised her standard to claim the English throne. Northumberland and Lady Jane Grey

were both beheaded and papacy returned to England. John
Aubrey tells how the nuns, led by their Abbess, returned to Wilton
and Earl William fell upon his knees, his cap in his hand, crying
out 'Peccavi. I have sinned'. On the death of Mary, however,
'The Earl fell upon the nuns like a tigyre and drove them out,
crying "Out ye whores. To work, to work ye whores, go spinne"'.

His son Henry succeeded as second earl, 'turning Wilton into
an academie as well as a palace'. He continued the building his
father had begun and spent vast sums on pictures and books. His
third wife was the beautiful and gifted daughter of Sir Henry
Sidney. Together she and her brother, Sir Philip Sidney, brought
some of the most distinguished men of letters to Wilton House.
Here her brother wrote his *Arcadia*, and together they translated
the Psalms into English metre.

Tragedy cruelly struck at the countess, for in one year she lost
her father, her mother, and finally her beloved brother. This last
loss was a crushing blow from which she never really recovered,
though she continued to act as his literary executrix. Her marriage
became estranged and on his death the earl 'left her as bare as a
board'. She seems to have become highly salacious, for that
inimitable gossip John Aubrey wrote:

> She was a beautiful ladie and had an excellent witt. She was very
> salacious and had in her garden a contrivance that in the spring of
> the yeare when the stallions were used to leape the mares, they
> were to be brought before such a part of the house where she had
> a vidette (a hole to peepe out at) to look on them and please her-
> selfe with their sport, and then she would act the like sport
> herselfe with her stallions.

William, third earl, was according to Clarendon 'immediately
given up to women' and was quite early in trouble with Queen
Elizabeth for making her favourite maid-of-honour, Mary Fitton,
pregnant. He was at once imprisoned in the Fleet prison and
banished from court. He came back into favour again, however,
under James I. He was immensely interested in the New World
and became a member of the King's Council for Virginia,
Bermuda and Guiana. He was also a man of great culture and

patron of many poets, among them Donne, Massinger, and Chapman, and sent Ben Jonson an annual gift of £20 to buy books. Both he and his brother were friends and patrons of Shakespeare who dedicated his First Folio 'to the most noble and incomparable pair of brethren William and Philip Herbert'.

His brother who succeeded him as fourth earl was surly, choleric, quarrelsome, uncouth and foul-mouthed, according to contemporary historians. In spite of all these faults his handsome and comely appearance soon attracted James I, always on the alert for any masculine beauty to satisfy his peculiar tastes, who showered honours and titles on him. He granted him Trinidad, Tobago, and the Barbadoes, and created him Baron Herbert of Shurland in the Isle of Sheppey, Kent, Knight of the Garter, and first Earl of Montgomery. In return for these favours he entertained James I for months on end at Wilton in a round of hawking, hunting and orgies.

He found equal favour under Charles I 'who did love Wilton of all places', and went every summer there. The king, himself a great connoisseur and one of the first and best buyers of pictures in England, was extremely influential in his advice to the earl, making Wilton the very beautiful place it is today. The queen, however, disliked the earl intensely and became a bitter enemy. He had angered Charles by his recommendation to accept the terms laid down by the Scots, voted against Strafford, and had such a violent quarrel with Lord Maltravers, son of the Earl of Arundel, that they were both confined to the Tower. The queen finally fulfilled her long-awaited revenge by having him dismissed from the high office of Lord Chamberlain.

He became a Parliamentarian and was one of the delegates appointed to receive the king's person from the Scots and conduct him to Holmby, for which service he was appointed Constable of Windsor Castle and Keeper of the Great Park. He was subtle enough not to become directly involved in the trial and execution of Charles I, but was not averse from watching him being led down Whitehall on the morning of his execution.

Philip, seventh earl, a tall, dark, powerfully built young man, in the space of a lifetime lasting only thirty years became the most violent homicide of his age, and according to one authority, responsible for no less than twenty-six crimes. He was only twenty-four when he killed a man in a duel and was dangerously wounded himself. He had scarcely recovered when he wooed and with suspicious haste married Henriette de Keroualle, youngest sister of the Duchess of Portsmouth the hated and notorious mistress of Charles II. After his daughter was born the earl left both her and her mother and began his life of drunken violence, brawling, beatings, duels and murders. After throwing a bottle of wine at the head of another nobleman the earl was soundly thrashed. He next killed a man named Vaughan, the second time in the family history that a Pembroke had killed a Vaughan. A week later, one Riccaut petitioned the House of Lords for protection after the earl's violent attempt to throttle him. Pembroke was bound over in the sum of £2,000 to keep the king's peace. One month later he appeared before a grand jury on a charge of murder, but claiming a peer's privilege was discharged with a very severe warning. The foreman of the jury who voted against him was later found brutally murdered in Leicester Fields, not far from Pembroke's London house.

Only two years after his acquittal, when on his way home, violently drunk and abusive, he was challenged by one Smeeth, in charge of the Chiswick Watch. Pembroke drew his sword and ran Smeeth through the stomach, leaving him to die. Incredible as it seems he once more pleaded a peer's privilege and received the king's pardon. Three months later he had a violent quarrel with the Earl of Dorset over some land, and laid violent hands on him. Dorset was saved from Pembroke's hastily drawn sword by his own servant. Once again Pembroke came before the House of Lords. Both were confined to their houses but Dorset accepted Pembroke's apologies the next morning, pleading 'he was in drink' and honour was satisfied. Pembroke went at once to Wilton which he never left again. There he drank himself steadily into a state of imbecility. His long-deserted wife came back to help him but he was far beyond it, and she left again to go into a convent.

He was only thirty when he died and was buried in Salisbury Cathedral, where so many of the family lie.

The eighth earl was known as the 'Architect Earl', and held some of the highest offices in the land under Queen Anne and George I, of which one was the appointment of Lord High Admiral. He was a connoisseur on the grand scale, and passionately collected gems, bought the Arundel marbles, and was a great patron of poets. He married the heiress of Sir Robert Sawyer of Highclere, Hampshire, the collateral line of the Carnarvon Herberts.

His son, Henry, ninth earl, born into great wealth and culture, was a patrician in all its senses. He said he could walk twenty miles faster than a coach and horses, and was a redoubtable and ferocious pugilist, no doubt inheriting much of his scurrilous grandfather's violence. He was also an appalling swearer and blasphemer, with an ungovernable and frightening temper, rude and quarrelsome, yet having a reputation for never bearing malice and being extremely kind. His architectural achievements were many and various, but principally Marble Hall at Twickenham, the White Lodge in Richmond Park, and the exquisite Palladian bridge over the Nadder at Wilton House.

Henry, tenth earl, had none of his father's taste and skill, but his passion for horses led him to build a riding school at Wilton. He married a daughter of the Duke of Marlborough. Shortly after he eloped to Holland with another woman, implored his wife to come over and live with them *à trois*, and came back alone. With generations of inherited virility he littered the continent with bastards.

The present seventeenth Earl of Pembroke and fourteenth Earl of Montgomery has made an outstanding name for himself as a film director, winning an Oscar in 1973 for his sensitive and understanding study of blind children. In addition to his many titles he holds the baronies of Shurland and Lea, and the ancient baronies in fee of Ross of Kendal, Parr, Marmion and St Quintin.

KILLIGREW

Arms: Argent, a double headed eagle displayed sable within a bordure of the second besantee.

Though the origins of this very ancient Cornish family are obscure, they have left behind three outstanding monuments: the great port of Falmouth which they founded, the Lizard lighthouse which they originally set up, and Drury Lane Theatre in London which they built.

In almost 600 years of their eventful family history they have produced many pirates, one of them a woman, successive naval and military commanders, captains of Pendennis Castle, the great Tudor fortress guarding Falmouth, ambassadors, dramatists, wits, and rakes.

A number of them are buried in Westminster Abbey; there are monumental brasses in the Cornish churches of St Budock and St Gluvias, and a superb and massive silver loving cup, dated 1633, used annually by each successive mayor of Penryn. The senior male line became extinct when Sir Peter, the second baronet, died in 1704, his son George having been killed in a tavern brawl at Penryn in 1687.

The fine old sixteenth-century family mansion, Arwenack House, overlooking Falmouth harbour, with its bow window through which the Killigrews would watch like cats every sheltering ship as potential booty, still partly stands. Opposite is the tall granite obelisk to the memory of Sir Peter Killigrew, erected by Martin Lister, who took the name of Killigrew by marriage.

The first recorded Killigrew was Raphe, who held lands in Cornwall at St Erme during the reign of Henry III. The family historian, however, claims they were descended from an illegitimate child born to Richard, Earl of Cornwall, King of the Romans and brother of Henry III, by his concubine Jane de Valletorte. This may well account for the arms, the eagle being the Imperial Roman eagle, and the *bordure bezanty* indicating royal illegitimacy.

In 1385, some four generations later, Simon Killigrew married Jane, daughter and heiress of the Lord of Arwenack, whose rich lands lay between the Helford river and the Pendennis peninsula. Here the Killigrews settled, profiting by the fast growing trade of Penryn as a seaport.

Four more generations passed and the head of the line was John, whose monumental brass, and that of his son, are in St Budock church. He was, like all his descendants, a man of ferocious temper, indomitable will, great personal courage, not overtroubled by any moral scruples, ruthless, in turn rich and poor.

He it was who first saw the advantages of piracy and soon became involved as an 'aider'. He broke all established rules and raided his neighbours' property with arrogant inpunity, damaging their crops and stealing their horses and cattle. He was summoned no less than five times to the dreaded Star Chamber for violation of the king's peace. Even at the age of seventy he was formidable, and threatened to kill a Privy Council messenger who had come to his manor house to claim back six rubies which, he said, John's son Peter had stolen. He was so terrified by the violent outburst of Killigrew that he rushed empty handed from the house.

With his ill-gotten gains on land and sea, Killigrew rebuilt Arwenack Manor in 1567, the most costly house in Cornwall,

with a great banqueting hall with the large bow window overlooking the harbour of Falmouth. He surrounded the house with
walls, gardens, and extensive parklands, and built a secret and
private way reaching direct to the harbour.

He married Elizabeth Trewinnard of St Erth, near St Ives, the
first of many great and lucrative family marriages, the most important of which was probably that of his daughter Margaret to
Sir Francis Godolphin, whose taste for piracy only equalled his
own. Killigrew was a devout Protestant when his nefarious duties
allowed him time, and high in favour with Henry VIII, who in-
structed the Bishop of Exeter to give 'our manor of Penryn
Foreign and Minster to John Killigrew'. He also appointed him
first Captain of Pendennis Castle.

This formidable castle, with 100 cannon, was built by Henry
VIII against invasion on Killigrew's own land, high up on the
western headland guarding the entrance to the Fal and its great
harbour. It was one of a chain of maritime castles built round the
English coast. The views from its central keep are superb, and
not even a rowing boat could escape notice at any angle. It is a
favourite place today for holiday tourists. Opposite, at St Mawes,
was another castle, and Penryn already had its own blockade
stakes and chains across the creek to protect it from raiding pirates.

John died in 1567 leaving five sons and four daughters. The
fourth son, Sir Henry, and his brother Sir William, became
ancestors of the two cadet lines. Both were brilliant men who
played a considerable part in the history of those times. Sir
Henry's life was so full of incidents that a whole book has been
written about him alone. He was described as 'a rebel', was
learned, artistic, a fine painter and musician, and an outstanding
diplomatist. Queen Elizabeth was quick to notice and employ his
various talents, sending him on many missions abroad and to
Scotland to Mary Queen of Scots 'for the preservation of our
amity' as Elizabeth tartly put it. It is recorded that after the
murder of Darnley Sir Henry mysteriously gave the Queen of
Scots 'a message in a dark chamber'. He was knighted in France
in 1591 by the Earl of Essex. He was married twice and held the

wedding ceremony both times in the same London church. His magnificent and costly house in Lothbury in the City of London almost ruined him. He died in 1603.

Sir William, ancestor of the second cadet line, had a number of distinguished descendants. He died in 1622 and was succeeded by his son Sir Robert who was Vice-Chamberlain to Queen Henrietta Maria. He was appointed Captain of Pendennis Castle for life and seems to have served two terms in the Fleet prison for no known reason. He married Mary Woodhouse and had a large brood of children. His eldest daughter Anne was drowned in the Queen's barge whilst shooting London Bridge and was buried in Westminster Abbey.

His eldest son, Sir William, was Gentleman Usher to Charles I and Captain of Pendennis Castle. His fourth son was Thomas, jester, wit, dramatist, rake, and personal friend of Charles II. The king would see him at any time, even keeping ministers waiting to do so, because he loved his brilliant, witty, and always ribald conversation.

He once put a message under the king's plate before sitting down to dinner. It simply said 'All'. When the king asked for an explanation Thomas answered, 'The country has sent all, the city has lost all, the Court spent all, and if we don't mind all it will be the worse for us all.' On another occasion Louis XIV pointed out to him a picture at Versailles showing Christ crucified between two other pictures, one of himself, the other of the Pope. Thomas replied, 'I thank your Majesty for the explanation. I had heard that our Saviour was crucified between two thieves, but I never knew who they were until now.'

Charles II appointed him Resident at Venice, where Killigrew at once began to spend money lavishly both for himself and his master. He led a life of such debauchery that complaints made by the Venetian ambassador compelled a most reluctant Charles to recall his favourite. As compensation he appointed him Groom of the Bedchamber, with a royal grant to erect two new play-houses in London and raise two new companies of players to fill them.

Thus it was that Drury Lane Theatre was built in 1663, and known as the Theatre Royal. It was burned down in 1672 and rebuilt in 1674 by Wren. Killigrew himself acted in his own play. He married twice and was buried in Westminster Abbey, the king himself paying £50 towards the funeral expenses. Of his three legitimated sons Charles became Master of the Revels and Patentee of Drury Lane Theatre, leaving it on his death to his son.

The most notorious figure of the whole Killigrew family, senior and cadet lines, was Sir John of Arwenack. Piracy was in his blood, so too was any other method of obtaining money, by whatever means. Sir John was to marry a woman who became more notorious and disreputable than he was and together they set up an infamous partnership in piracy unequalled even in Cornwall in those times.

One of his relatives was Vice-Admiral of South Wales and controlled the Welsh side of the various ventures. Another relative, John Godolphin acted as Cornish agent, and yet another relative looked after the Irish side of the business from his base at Tralee. To make everything watertight Sir John himself was elected Chairman of the Commissioners of Piracy in Cornwall.

From the start of this new venture everything seemed to fall into their hands in the way of loot and plunder. Lady Killigrew, 'that Cornish Messalina' as she was called, held open house at Arwenack for other agents, accomplices, and 'aiders', and it was not long before a very rich prize indeed fell into her hands, though by overplaying her hand this time she brought a halt to the nefarious undertakings of the Killigrews.

It was on New Year's Day 1582 when her ever watchful eyes at the bow window spotted a Hansa ship which had run for shelter from a storm into Falmouth harbour. It did not take her long to find out that the ship had a valuable cargo aboard. Filling a boat with heavily armed Killigrew retainers she not only led the party alongside but was the first to board the ship. The crew, surprised and alarmed at the sudden attack, were slaughtered and their bodies flung overboard. After Lady Killigrew had removed several bolts of valuable holland cloth and two whole hogsheads of pieces of eight the ship, steered by servants, sailed to Tralee to dispose of the rest of the booty.

When information of this high sea piracy came to the ears of the owners they immediately lodged a violent protest to the Commissioners of Piracy in Cornwall, but Sir John, its Chairman, blandly returned an open verdict as sufficient evidence was lacking. The owners took the matter to the Privy Council who ordered a fuller investigation to be made. This resulted in complete exposure of the whole business, including murder, and sentence was passed on the accused to be executed forthwith. Two of the retainers were hanged and only very powerful strings pulled by friends on behalf of Lady Killigrew procured her a last minute reprieve.

When Lady Killigrew's servants were at the gallows, they 'lamented nothing more than that they had not the company of "that old Jezebel Killigrew at that place" and begged Almighty God that some remarkable judgement might befal her and her posterity, and all those who were instrumental in procuring her pardon'.

Sir John's grandson, another Sir John, was to follow out an idea his father had always had of building a Cornish lighthouse, and so it was that in 1619 Sir John built what has always been considered the first English lighthouse at the Lizard. He maintained, with his tongue in his cheek, that he did so for a charitable purpose in order to help ships at sea and to expect voluntary contributions from them for doing so. He at once infuriated the local inhabitants, and especially the powerful Basset family landowners, 'for taking away God's grace from them', as the salvage from wrecks was locally called and which brought rich plunder, as 'wreckers' soon found out by flashing false indication lights to lure ships on to the rocks.

Sir John, completely ignoring all their protests, continued with his plan, the cost of coal alone being 10s a night, and by 1620 he had spent over £500 without receiving a penny from the passing ships. So the light went out and 'God's grace' returned for good, or so the locals thought. They did not know Sir John, however, who by pressure in all directions had succeeded in obtaining authority for a fixed contribution from all passing ships. So the light went on once again, this time for ten years, when the ealous oppositio n of Trinity House finally forced the light out for good. The present Lizard lighthouse was erected in 1751, but coal fires continued to be used until 1812.

Sir John had married Jane Fermor, the daughter of Sir George Fermor of Northampton, but because of accusations reaching his ears of her debauchery with Sir Nicholas Parker, he obtained a divorce. Lady Jane took refuge at a lodging house in St Thomas Street, Penryn. In gratitude to the town for protecting her she presented it with the massive silver loving cup, which is one of its most treasured possessions, inscribed 'From Maior to Maior to the towne of Permarin when they received mee that was in great misery—Jane Killygrew 1633.' The cup is held by each successive mayor after taking the statutory oath even to this day, though it is difficult to understand why Penryn ever accepted the gift in the first place, knowing what sort of a woman she was and where the silver probably came from.

Sir John died heavily in debt, whilst the two Killigrew cadet lines continued to thrive in great prosperity with honours showered upon them. Of his two brothers, Sir William was created a baronet in 1660, and after having wasted the whole of his father's estate and alienating Arwenack Manor to his brother Peter, he died and was quite unaccountably buried in Westminster Abbey. This Peter was known as 'Peter the Post' for his great diligence in carrying messages to and from Charles I during the Civil Wars. He was succeeded by his son Sir Peter, who, through his uncle William became the second baronet, the notorious Sir John having died without issue.

It was in the year 1687 that George, son of Sir Peter the second baronet, was killed in a Penryn tavern brawl, when he was drunk and quarrelsome, as the Killigrews so often were. His assailant was a barrister named Walter Vincent, who though acquitted, it was said through bribery, never recovered from the shock of his act. He lived for two more years, finally collapsing and dying at table in the Bishop of Exeter's palace in the presence of a number of people, many of whom called it 'a judgement of God'.

George's father died in Ludlow in 1704, his body being brought back to Falmouth in Cornwall for burial in the parish church of King Charles the Martyr, and the senior male line became extinct after almost 500 years. Anne, the younger sister of George, married Martin Lister of Staffordshire in 1727; he assumed the name and arms of Killigrew and became the family historian. The elder sister, Frances, married Richard Erisey, and their great-granddaughter Sophia married Lord Wodehouse, of a very ancient family, from whom the extant line of the earldom of Kimberley descends.

LOVEL

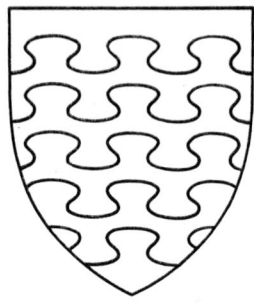

Arms: Barry nebuly of six, or and gules.

Every year hundreds of people visit the gaunt, melancholy ruins of Minster Lovell Hall, once the home of the ill-fated Lovel, or Lovell family. It is between Burford and Witney in Oxfordshire, in the beautiful Windrush valley, and is backed by the line of trees of Wychwood Forest.

The mansion and the nearby church were built by William, seventh Baron Lovel, in 1430, and even in its present state is an outstanding example of medieval domestic architecture. The ruins consist mainly of the west tower, a fifty-foot high stately banqueting hall with a central fireplace, four finely detailed great windows, and a vaulted passage. Outside is the medieval pigeon loft or dovecote.

The mansion was built on the site of a small priory attached to Ivry Abbey in Normandy; the word 'Minster' prefixing the family name was used to commemorate this ancient religious house. To the west is the aisleless, cruciform church where its founder lies on a splendid fifteenth-century alabaster tomb in the south transept. He is clad in plate armour, his sword at his side, and there are shields bearing the family arms. He died on 14 June 1455, aged fifty-eight, and before his death left strict orders that the family arms, *barry nebuly of six, or and gules* were not only to be displayed in armorial glass but even on the rood loft.

The diarist Richard Symonds, when he was campaigning here in the Civil War, wrote of the effigy: 'His body compleate armour of woove worke yet somewhat like the Black Prince'. In the year 1900 it was falling into ruin, the tomb foundations had sunk at one end and the figure was broken across the middle. It was carefully restored at the expense of the Earl of Egmont, a collateral descendant of the Lovel family.

There is one more link with the family in the church; this is a brass to John Vampage in the south transept. He was 'attorney in the King's cases', and came as a Royal Commissioner to Minster Lovell to supervise the taking over of the estates after the mysterious disappearance of Francis, the ninth baron.

The Lovels descended from an ancient Norman family, the first of whom came over with William the Conqueror, and was granted the feudal lordship of Castle Cary in Somerset as a reward for his services. It has been said that one of these ancestors had such a dangerous and violent temper that he was known as Lupus, 'the Wolf'. His son, inheriting it also, was known as 'Lupellus' or 'Little Wolf'. This became Lupel, then Lovel or Lovell.

In the year 1241 Philip Lovel was the guardian to the Jews, Henry III being on the throne, and was 'charged with great bribery in taking plate of much value to exempt some of them from the tallage then imposed'. Through powerful influence at Court he made his peace with the king and got off with a heavy fine of 11,000 marks. So well did he win back the royal favour that the king very surprisingly appointed him Treasurer of England, a most ill-considered and unpopular choice. The barons were incensed and demanded his trial and dismissal from office. The king was forced not only to comply but to impose an even heavier penalty, as well as seizing all the Lovel estates for the crown until that penalty should be discharged. This punishment and loss of royal favour so afflicted Lovel that he died, it is said, 'of grief and vexation at his own rectory having previously taken orders'.

The first Baron Lovel was created in 1299, and inherited the very considerable Tichmersh estates in Northamptonshire, brought to his father when he married the very rich heiress Maud Sydenham. The baron was allowed the high privilege of castellating the Tichmersh mansion, and also allowed to hold a weekly market and an annual fair.

John, the fifth baron, was created a Knight of the Garter by Richard II. By his marriage to Maud, daughter and heir of Robert de Holand, his title became Baron Lovel and Holand.

William, seventh baron, increased the family wealth still further by marrying Alice, granddaughter of Lord Grey of Rotherfield, co-heiress to the Deincourt barony, thus uniting the four baronies of Lovel, Holand, Grey of Rotherfield, and Deincourt. So his full achievement of arms as shown on his Garter stall-plate was therefore: *quarterly; 1 barry nebuly of six pieces or and gules*, for Lovel; *2 azure, seme of billets and a fess dancetty or*, for Deincourt; *3 azure, seme of fleurs de lys and a lion rampant argent*, for Holand (or Holland); *4 barry of six pieces argent and azure, a bend gules, over all an inescutcheon argent and a lion rampant crowned sable holding an acorn between the paws*, Grey of Rotherfield.

This enormous wealth no doubt motivated his desire to build a great and splendid mansion becoming his high rank and titles, and in the year 1430 he began to build Minster Lovell Hall, which he only lived in for twenty-five years before he died. It was in the fateful year 1455 when the Wars of the Roses broke out and split England down the middle, ending with the final extinction of the Plantagenet line and the creation of the great Tudor dynasty. John, eighth Baron Lovel was soon involved, for hearing of the landing of the Duke of York, he hurried to London with the Lords Scales and Hungerford to stir up the citizens in favour of the luckless Henry VI, but was forced to seek sanctuary in the Tower. Shortly afterwards the Yorkist cause prevailed throughout England to the total ruin of the king. John Lovel died in the second year of Edward IV's reign, lucky enough to keep his estates and, what is more, his head, in those bloody and bitter days.

His son Francis succeeded as ninth baron, and in the two short, eventful years of Richard III's reign he attained some of the highest honours in the land. Almost as soon as he was crowned Richard created Lovel a viscount and Lord Chamberlain. Later he was made Constable of Wallingford Castle, and Chief Butler of England.

Very soon the Lancastrians had issued an insinuating and widely spread couplet, which cost the writer his head:

> When the Cat, the Rat, and Lovel the Dog
> All ruled England under the Hog

The Cat was Catesby, the Rat Ratcliff, and the Dog was taken from Lovel's crest of a silver wolf dog, allusive to his ancestor's nickname of Lupellus, with a gold coronet around its neck. His badge was a square padlock. The Hog was Richard III.

Sir William Catesby bore *Argent, two lions passant sable each with a crown or*. His badge was a white cat spotted with black and wearing a gold collar. He was beheaded after Bosworth.

Sir Richard Ratcliff, second son of Sir Thomas Ratcliff of Derwentwater bore *Argent, a bend engrailed sable, with a crescent for difference*. He was slain at Bosworth.

Lovel had married at an extremely early age, Anna, daughter of Baron Fitz-Hugh. He fought with Richard III at Bosworth Field, and was lucky enough to escape with his life after learning of his sovereign's defeat and death by Henry VII. He knew now that, like so many other Yorkists, he was a hunted man. He first fled to Colchester, then to Lancashire where he sought refuge in Sir John Broughton's house. From here he raised a revolt in the north which very nearly resulted in the capture of the new king at York, but ended disastrously.

He at once set sail for Flanders and was hospitably received by Margaret, Duchess of Burgundy, the late King Richard's widowed sister. She it was who placed him at the head of 2,000 troops to go to Ireland in support of the Yorkist pretender Lambert Simnel, who claimed to be Edward, Earl of Warwick, son of the late

king's elder brother, the Duke of Clarence, and therefore the
lawful king of England. From Ireland Lovel landed in Lancaster
in 1481 and marched towards York at the head of some 2,000
German mercenaries and wild Irish foot soldiers armed only with
darts. Near Stoke they met head on with Henry VII's trained and
disciplined army who cut the rebel forces down like a field of ripe
corn.

Once again the luckless Lovel escaped with his life, and was last
seen swimming his horse across the Trent but unable to find a
landing place on the opposite bank owing to its steepness. From
that moment Viscount Lovel completely vanished from existence,
though not from history, and his legendary end was as dramatic
as anything ever recorded.

In the reign of Henry VIII it became necessary to secure evidence of his death for the legal dispersal of his property. A jury
established that he had escaped beyond the sea and died abroad,
but their verdict was not based on any actual evidence. Indeed,
there were many people living near Minster Lovell who had never
believed this, for rumours had quickly circulated that Viscount
Francis had secretly found his way back there and hidden somewhere in his own great mansion until he thought it safe to emerge
again.

Almost 200 years later the poet William Cowper, then Clerk of
the Parliament, wrote a singularly disquieting letter from Herting-
fordbury Park, dated 9 August 1747.

Sir, I met t'other day with a memorandum I had made some years
ago perhaps not unworthy of notice. You may remember that
Lord Bacon in his "History of Henry the Seventh" giving an
account of the battle of Stoke, says of the Lord Lovel who was
among the rebels, that he fled and swam over the Trent on horseback but could not recover the further side by reason of the steepness of the bank, and so was drowned in the river. But another
report leaves him not there but that he lived long after in a cave or
vault. Apropos to this on the 6th May, 1728, the present Duke of
Rutland stated in my hearing that about twenty years before,
viz., in 1708, upon occasion of laying a new chimney at Minster
Lovell there was discovered a large vault underground in which

was the entire skeleton of a man as having been sitting at a table which was before him, with a book, paper, pen, &c.; in another part of the room lay a cap, all much mouldered and decayed. Which the family and others judged to be this Lord Lovel whose exit has hitherto been so uncertain.

The mystery of Lovel's death has never been explained. It seems reasonably certain from the slender evidence available that he managed to return to his home where perhaps a trusted servant hid him in the room where he was found sitting, but it will never be known if the servant, who alone had the key, either died or betrayed his master by leaving him immured in his living tomb, to starve to death.

An even stranger story is the appearance, a few years later, of a man known as Rustling Jack, who claimed to be the viscount's former valet and who, after the battle of Stoke, had fled to Spain. He said that the Lovel treasure was also hidden with its master. Four people, one a monk, set out to find this treasure, and armed with picks and shovels they found the secret chamber where the skeleton of Viscount Lovel sat at the table. Whether they found the treasure will never be known, but before their horrified eyes the skeleton suddenly crumbled to a pile of dust.

Immediately after Lovel's disappearance and supposed death by drowning Henry VII added a final twist to the family tragedy. Under an Act of Attainder he confiscated the whole of the vast estates and wealth for the crown, especially Minster Lovell Hall, 'that mansion inferior to none in my kingdom'. It was, as Banks wrote 'a melancholy period indeed to the life and fortunes of one of the greatest and most active noblemen of the era wherein he had lived'.

Under the attainder the four baronies of Lovel, Holand, Deincourt and Grey of Rotherfield fell into abeyance and could not be inherited by the viscount's sisters, and thus the line terminated, there being no male heir to succeed.

The Barony of Lovel and Holland of Enmore, Somerset, is now vested in the Earl of Egmont, who is also a Baronet of Ireland amongst many other titles.

NEVILL OF RABY

Earls of Westmoreland

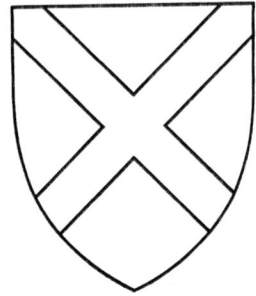

Arms: Gules, a saltire argent.

Two splendidly preserved castles in County Durham, a third in ruins in Yorkshire, and churches in both counties filled with their tombs and monuments, are abundant evidence of the former power and wealth of the Nevills of Raby, Earls of Westmoreland.

Castle Raby in County Durham stands today in magnificent splendour within its 270 acres of parkland, of which no less than nine acres are lakes. Its finest individual feature is the mighty 132ft long Barons Hall in which Lord John Nevill, according to Sir Walter Scott's *Rokeby*, could assemble 'seven hundred knights retainers all of Nevill at their master's call'.

Another fine feature is the impressive castle gatehouse guarding the drawbridge, with its portcullis grooves and massive door. Behind is Clifford's Tower, one of the four impregnable towers punctuating the soaring plain walls of the castle itself, 80ft high and 10ft thick, containing some of the original loopholes and windows. Beyond a short curtain wall is Mount Raskelf Tower, named after one of the Nevill's Yorkshire manors, with four roof turrets. In the south-east corner is the five-sided Bulmer's Tower, so named after the former owners of Brancepeth Castle who married into the Nevill family. Joan's Tower, much modernised, was named after Joan Beaufort, John of Gaunt's daughter, who married Ralph Nevill.

The outstanding feature of the whole west front of the castle, however, is the stately Nevill gateway to the inner court, where stands the original keep and flight of stone steps leading to the Rose of Raby room, named after Cecily Nevill, mother of Edward IV and Richard III.

Their two other great castles were the nearby Brancepeth, still in fine preservation and now used as a research laboratory, and Middleham in the North Riding of Yorkshire, on the banks of the river Ure.

As if all this were not sufficient evidence of their former greatness there is, in Durham Cathedral, the exceedingly beautiful Nevill Screen, the gift of John, third Lord Nevill of Raby. It was carved in London in about 1372, shipped to Newcastle and taken by cart to the cathedral. Originally there were no less than 107 niche statues adorning it. These, however, were all destroyed by the Scottish Presbyterians imprisoned in the cathedral after the battle of Dunbar. Strangely enough, the extreme beauty of the remaining screen is unimpaired and all the damaged stone pinnacles were carefully restored.

In the village of Staindrop, where Raby Castle stands, a considerable number of monuments to the Nevill family are to be seen in the church. Indeed, it is one of the most impressive collections of monuments in County Durham, most of them being to the various lords and ladies who lived and died in Raby Castle. The oldest of them is said to be that of Elizabeth FitzMaldred, who died about 1260. There is another to Euphemia Clavering, mother of the second baron, Ralph Nevill, victor of Nevill's Cross, who built the south aisle of the church. At the west end of the aisle lies Ralph, first Earl of Westmoreland, on top of a once magnificent but now much battered alabaster tomb. He wears the Lancastrian SS collar and has a richly embroidered sword belt. He was grandfather of Warwick 'the Kingmaker'. Another remarkable tomb is that of the fifth earl who died in 1564. Under the tower is a font bearing the Nevill arms, *Gules, a saltire argent*.

In Brancepeth church also are some beautiful monuments, all executed under the patronage of the Nevills. The most impressive is that of Robert, 'the Peacock of the North', who died in 1318 and lies here in his armour and surcoat. On the other side of the church are fine oak figures of the second earl, 'a man of peace', with one of his two wives.

In their 400 years of existence they did much to shape the whole course of English history. 'The Nevills were to England what the Douglas was to Scotland', wrote a contemporary historian. Another, recording the death of Richard Nevill, Earl of Warwick, 'the Kingmaker', wrote, 'He was the greatest and last of the old Norman chivalry, more kinglike in pride, in state, in possessions, and in renown than the king himself.'

It is indeed doubtful if any English family has ever surpassed them in honours, titles, wealth and alliances. Their impressive pedigree includes six Earls of Westmoreland, two Earls of Salisbury, one of them the Earl of Warwick, 'the Kingmaker', nineteen Barons, five Earls of Abergavenny, one Earl of Kent, ten Marquesses of Montacute, one of whom was also Duke of Bedford, five Barons Latimer, one Lord Furnival, and one Lord Fauconberg. There were also two Archbishops of York, two Lord High Chancellors, nine Knights of the Garter, and one Speaker.

In Lord Lytton's fine novel, *The Last of the Barons*, he speaks of the annual income of Richard Nevill, Earl of Warwick, as exceeding £300,000, a fabulous sum of money today. He writes also:

> His wealth was enormous but it was equalled by his magnificence and rendered popular by his lavish hospitality. No less than 30,000 persons are stated to have feasted daily at the open tables with which he allured to his countless castles the strong hands and grateful hearts of a martial and unsettled population.

The Nevill women were scarcely less distinguished, since they produced one Queen of England, a mother of two English monarchs, and seven duchesses. Of Anne Nevill's unhappy marriage with Richard III enough is known, but few families could have equalled in tragedy the life of Cecily Nevill, the youngest of twenty-three children the virile first earl engendered from two wives. She was married to the Duke of York who was killed in battle, her second son was murdered, her eldest cut down in the prime of his life and his two sons reputedly butchered by their uncle Richard III. After thirty-five years of widowhood she was buried at Fotheringhay in Northamptonshire.

The head of the Nevill line was Gilbert, admiral of William the Conqueror's fleet for the conquest of England. His grandson Geoffrey married Emma, daughter of Bertram de Bulmer, Lord of Brancepeth, which on his death brought this great castle into the Nevill family. Their daughter Isabel married Robert FitzMaldred, the Saxon lord of Raby, who upon his marriage took the name of Nevill of Raby. These two impregnable castles became known as the castles of war and festival, Raby being the former, the Nevills always preferring Brancepeth, perhaps because it was nearer to Durham.

The third great castle of Middleham in Yorkshire came to the family when Robert Nevill married Mary, daughter and sole heiress of Ralph FitzRanulf, or FitzRandolph, Lord of Middleham. It was in this castle that 'Crouchback', Duke of Gloucester, later Richard III, wooed and won Anne Nevill. Here, in this great gloomy castle the unhappy Anne spent her married life, giving birth to her son Edward, the place where he was born being still called 'The Prince's Tower'.

Ralph Nevill, the first baron, created in 1294, cared little for this vast wealth and preferred a monastic life with the monks of Coverham, and on his death was buried there. During his lifetime he had a long and bitter feud with the Prior of Durham to whom, on St Cuthbert's Day, he paid an annual rent of £4 and a stag, for ownership of certain land. Nevill demanded that the stag should be killed and served to him and all his retinue by his own servants in the abbey, the monks absenting themselves for the day, and that he, the Lord Nevill of Raby, should be lodged for the night and served breakfast next day. The Prior angrily refused to invite him to dinner or absent the monks. The dispute was still unresolved at the time of Nevill's death in 1331.

He married twice, and by his first wife Euphemia Clavering had two sons. Robert, the elder, from his love of finery and ostentation was known as 'the Peacock of the North'; he later died in a border skirmish.

His brother Ralph, who succeeded as second baron was of a totally different character, warlike, a skilful diplomat, and immensely proud. His greatest feat was his victory at Nevill's Cross, in October 1346, when King David of Scotland was defeated and captured. He had revived his father's feud with the Prior over the stag, threatening to appeal to the country if the Prior continued to refuse to acknowledge his lawful claim. Nevill insisted absolutely that they should go once only through the whole original ceremony but with modifications. Instead of bringing a retinue he brought only his wine butler, his cook, and one servant to admit him whilst the monks absented themselves. He thereafter dined, but left a servant to stay the night and to have breakfast on part of the stag. Honour was satisfied on both sides and Nevill asserted his ancient rights.

He was the first layman to be buried in Durham Cathedral, granted to him as a favour, it was said, for his gift 'of an investment of red velvet tasselled with gold and rich with figures of saints in tabernacles, given by him to St Cuthbert'. His body was brought in a chariot drawn by seven horses to as far as the boundary, then borne by knights to the centre of the church. At the Mass eight fully caparisoned horses were offered as sacrifice, four men armed with all their accoutrements accompanying them to the altar. Four of the horses were redeemed by the dead lord's son and heir for 100 marks, plus gold hangings and damask silk.

John, third Lord Nevill, fought with distinction in Turkey, was made High Admiral and a Knight of the Garter. He was such a distinguished soldier that John of Gaunt retained him in his service for life. He made a powerful alliance with the great de Percy family of Northumberland by marrying Maud, daughter of Lord Henry, first Earl of Northumberland. Before his death in 1388 Nevill built the great Barons Hall in Raby Castle, and was later buried in Durham Cathedral, close to his father, the second layman only to be thus interred.

His son Ralph had many great honours conferred upon him. He was successively Constable of the Tower of London, Earl Marshal of England, Earl of Richmond for life, Governor of Carlisle, Warden of the Marches and Forests towards Scotland, Governor of Roxburgh, Knight of the Garter, and created first Earl of Westmoreland. He married firstly Lady Margaret Stafford by whom he had a son who predeceased him, and secondly Joan Beaufort, daughter of Katherine Swynford and John of Gaunt, Duke of Lancaster. Such was the earl's virility that he fathered no less than twenty-three children by his two wives. Three of his sons became Earl of Salisbury, Earl of Kent, and Baron Latimer respectively, and a fourth marrying Lady Elizabeth Beauchamp, became ancestor of the Earls of Abergavenny.

His eldest son by his first marriage having predeceased him, his grandson Ralph succeeded as fifth Baron Nevill of Raby and second Earl of Westmoreland. He also made a distinguished marriage into the de Percy family by marrying Elizabeth, daughter of the renowed 'Hotspur'. Their son having predeceased both parents, the title was taken by the nephew of the second earl, also named Ralph 'who died of grief at the loss of his own son'.

The title then passed to the grandson, yet another Ralph. He was high in favour at the court of Henry VIII and was one of the signatories of the letter to the Pope regarding the divorce of Catherine of Aragon, for which he was made a Knight of the Garter.

He married Lady Catherine Stafford by whom he had a son, Henry, who succeeded him. Henry also was made a Knight of the Garter and married Lady Anne Manners, by whom he had fourteen children, the eldest of whom succeeded him as sixth Earl of

Westmoreland. He it was who finally brought the great line of Nevill of Raby to an end by one single act of rash folly, which from the start was ill-planned, rushed, and fated to disaster.

In the year 1569 the earl received at Brancepeth Castle Henry Percy, ninth Earl of Northumberland, and together they planned the 'Rising of the North', whereby the two earls, with very considerable united forces, were to restore Papacy to England by placing Mary, Queen of Scots on the throne.

The coup resulted in total defeat and disaster. Percy was captured, imprisoned in the Tower and later murdered by three pistol shots from an unknown assailant. Nevill fled to Scotland where he sought protection and concealment in Roxburghshire at Fernyhurst Castle.

Sir Ralph Sadleir, acting for the Government, sought to blackmail the earl's cousin, Robert Constable, to locate the earl's hiding place, and after making contact, betray him. This plan emerged from the Sadleir State Papers, summed up by Burke as 'an immense memorial of treachery and baseness'. The earl, having information of this plot, fled at once from Scotland to Flanders. Under an Act of Attainder all his vast lands, titles and honours were confiscated by the Crown, together with the three great castles of Raby, Brancepeth, and Middleham.

The exiled earl was penniless, so too were his wife Lady Jane Howard, daughter of the Earl of Surrey and sister of the Duke of Norfolk, and their four daughters, three of whom were married.

It was impossible for the exiled earl to get money from England, and three years after the disastrous 'Rising' he was living on a miserable pension in Flanders, granted to him by the Catholic King of Spain. Lord Seton even wrote to Mary, Queen of Scots personally, stating that 'the Earl of Westmoreland had neither penny nor halfpenny'.

The Bishop of Durham wrote to Lord Burghley, suing for the pardon of the earl's third daughter who had married Sir Nicholas Pudsey and was being humiliated and persecuted for her Catholic beliefs:

I sent up in the beginning of term to sue for the pardon of the Lady Margaret Nevill. She lamented with tears that she hath offended God and her sovereign. Dr. Aubrey hath had her pardon drawn since the beginning of term. If it come not quickly I fear she will die of sorrow. It were very honourable for your good lordship to take the case of a most distressed maydn, descended as your lordship knoweth of great nobilitie, the House of Norfolk, the House of Westmoreland, and the House of Rutland, and was but a child of five when her father did enter into rebellion. Now she is a condemned person having not one penny to live upon since the death of her mother who gave her £33. 6s. 8d a year, part of the £300 which Her Majesty did allow her. It was well that Her Majesty were informed of her miserable state.

For more than thirty years the exiled earl lived out his life of poverty in Flanders, dying penniless and unknown there in the year 1601. As there was no male heir the Nevills of Raby, in disgrace, ignominy, and poverty, became extinct.

During the reign of James I a claim was made by Edward Nevill to the barony of Raby and earldom of Westmoreland, but was not granted.

The head of the distinguished extant Nevill line is now the Marquess of Abergavenny, whose other titles are Earl of Lewes, Earl of Abergavenny, Viscount Nevill and Baron Abergavenny.

PAULET

Earls Poulett

Arms: Sable, three swords in pile, points in base argent, pommels and hilts or.

The Somerset village of Pawlett stands on the main Bridgwater road. Between that town and the sea stretch the 2,000 acres of rich pastureland known as the Pawlett Hams.

In 1134 all these lands and the manor were granted to a certain Picardy knight named Hercules Sieur de Tournan by Henry II as a reward for assisting him to win the throne from Stephen. The family, variously adopting the name of Paulet, Pawlett, Poulet or Poulett, remained here for over 300 years before acquiring through marriage the Norman manor of Hinton, now Hinton St George, near Crewkerne, also in Somerset, and where the senior line continued to live until the death of the eighth Earl Poulett in 1972.

If there are no traces at all of their existence at Pawlett there are none lacking in the church of Hinton St George. Here is one of the most extraordinary collection of family tombs to be seen in England. The Poulett pew and private chapel have an almost unbelievable, even melancholy assembly of alabaster and marble tombs of all shapes and sizes. The silver swords in their coats of arms have turned bright blue and they are everywhere, forty-eight of them on one tomb alone. There are effigies of knights, alone, and with their wives; and weepers, mottoes and epitaphs, one of them said to have been written by Queen Elizabeth herself and bearing her cipher initials above it; angels and satyrs supporting shields of arms; sphinxes, lions, medallions, putti, and acanthus leaves. There is even a stone to a family bailiff of sixty-two years' service who left, in 1792, a sum of £9 to buy shoes and stockings for the village poor for 1,000 years.

Near to the church is the family residence, Hinton House, recently sold and converted into flats, a large, irregular building. Though nothing exists of its original fifteenth-century architecture it was, in 1487 when Sir Amias Paulet built it, a low quadrangular building with square turrets at each angle.

The first recorded descendant of Hercules was Sir John Paulet of Pawlett and Gotehurst. He died in 1356. His son, another Sir John, fought in the French wars and married Elizabeth, daughter and heiress of Sir John Creedy of Creedy, Devon. There were two sons of this marriage, Sir Thomas who added a second 't' to the family name, and William, ancestor of the great line of Marquesses of Winchester, Earls of Wiltshire, and Dukes of Bolton.

Sir Thomas's son, also William, married Elizabeth, daughter and heiress of John Denehand, through whom the ancient Norman manor of Hinton came into possession of the Paulett family. He was later knighted by Henry VI and was succeeded by his son, the first Sir Amias. He it was who put the young rector of nearby Limington in the stocks 'for being scandalously drunk'. Unfortunately for Sir Amias the young rector became the powerful Cardinal Wolsey, who never forgave him for it and had his revenge by confining him to London for six whole years.

Sir Amias was knighted on the field after the battle of Stoke and the defeat of the imposter Perkin Warbeck. He was also one of the distinguished nobles appointed to escort Catherine of Aragon on her bridal journey through Somerset. He built part of the church and most of Hinton House, and though a reputedly rich country gentleman was said to have been heavily in debt to both Henry VII and Henry VIII.

He married firstly his cousin Margaret, daughter of Sir John Paulet of Nunney Castle. The additional title 'of Nunney' had come down from his great-grandfather William, ancestor of the Marquess of Winchester, who by marrying Eleanor, daughter and heiress of Philip de la Mare, had acquired the very important Somerset castle of Nunney, 3½ miles south-west of Frome. It was built by John de la Mare from ransom money he collected in the French wars, and in the year 1373 he received licence and privilege from Edward III to crenellate it. It is now a splendid ruin, listed as an ancient monument and open to the public.

As there was no issue from Sir Amias's first marriage, he married again, a Hampshire lady, by whom he is said to have had a son, Sir Hugh, Governor of Jersey. Sir Amias always signed his name as Poulet.

Sir Hugh's son by his second wife was another Sir Amias, who changed the family name to Poulett, which the senior Somerset line bears to this day. His qualities of diplomacy brought him not only the friendship of most of the leading statesmen of the day, but of Queen Elizabeth herself, who constantly used his services, wrote him letters, and finally the epitaph on his tomb. A large collection of letters between him and his sovereign were in the possession of the late Earl Poulett at Hinton House.

The chief event in his life, and indeed in the troubled history of those times, was his guardianship of Mary, Queen of Scots, as a prisoner of Queen Elizabeth at Tutbury. She protested most vigorously against his appointment, knowing him to be a most strict Puritan, with a fierce hatred for all Catholics and impossible to tempt or bribe at any price. In spite of his bitterness towards her, however, he carried out his duties as gaoler with strict integrity and honour, even though he bombarded Burghley and

Walsingham with letters urging her execution, which Queen Elizabeth refused to allow.

Instead, her cruel and wily secretary, Sir Francis Walsingham, proposed to Sir Amias that he suborn one of his servants to be bribed by Queen Mary and thus obtain damning evidence of her plotting against Queen Elizabeth. Sir Amias, with great courage, not only refused to do so but replied in a long letter of great strength, sorrow, and indignation. 'God forbid that I should make so fowle a shipwracke of my conscience, or leave so great a blot to my poor posteritie, to shed blood without law or warrant.' He then requests Walsingham's good mediation for Her Majesty's accustomed clemency.

When the Queen read the letter she called Sir Amias 'a dainty and precise fellow who would promise much but perform nothing'. Later her anger became greater. 'Yet there are others who would do it for my sake.' Her ingratitude for service by her subjects was frequent. Poulett, suffering from her parsimony as well, had to provide out of his own pocket for 127 persons: 36 soldiers, 51 personal attendants of Mary, and his own retinue. Eventually he was ordered to remove her to Fotheringhay, and after her execution there in 1587 his duties came to an end.

Elizabeth made him Chancellor of the Order of the Garter as a reward. He died in London in 1588, and was buried in St Martin-in-the-Fields, but when that church was rebuilt his remains and magnificent monument were removed to Hinton St George, where they now are.

Sir Amias was succeeded by his son, the autocratic Sir Anthony, Captain of the Guard to Queen Elizabeth. Acting as Governor of Jersey during his father's lifetime he now became Governor in his own right. He and his uncle George, Bailiff of Jersey, ruled the island with great severity, repressing the Catholic religion, which resulted in a special commission being sent from London to examine the grievances of the islanders. Sir Anthony married Catherine, only daughter of Sir Henry Norris, Baron Norris of Rycote, Oxfordshire. Their eldest son John, one of ten children, was elevated to the peerage in 1627 as first Baron Poulett of

Hinton St George. He was a great Royalist and devoted to Charles
I whom he entertained at Hinton House. After the king's death
he made his peace with Parliament but his estates were com-
pounded for nearly £8,000.

An interesting document is extant granting Lord Poulett permission to travel from London to Hinton with a retinue of six
servants. After the accession of Queen Anne, his great grandson
John was created Viscount Poulett of Hinton St George and first
Earl Poulett, KG. His fourth son was named Anne after the
queen who sponsored him.

Of the cadet line, Sir William, son of Sir John Paulet of
Nunney, was a most remarkable man, dearly beloved by Queen
Elizabeth. In 1428 Basing Castle in Hampshire had been inherited
by the Paulet family, and William began to build Basing House,
one of the most splendid mansions to be seen in England, receiving licence to crenellate the latter in 1531. Both castle and house
were almost totally ruined during the Civil Wars. Fuller, in his
Worthies of England, describes how William 'as a younger brother
bearing a crescent on his arms to prove it, and having wasted all
that was left him came to court on trust, where, upon the bare
stock of his wit, he trafficked so wisely and prospered so well that
he got, spent, and left more than any subject since the Conquest'.
Carlyle wrote of him 'as a magnificent kind of man whose best
bed excited the wonder of the world'.

Like the Vicar of Bray he survived four Tudor sovereigns and
died under a fifth, in itself a remarkable feat in days when heads
rolled easily, especially under Henry VIII. When asked how he
had contrived to hold his offices through so many changeable
years, he replied, 'By being a willow, not an oak'. He held a
considerable number of important offices under each successive
sovereign, the most curious of which was 'Surveyor of the king's
widows and Governor of all idiots and naturals in the king's
hands'.

His two most unpleasant duties were firstly to go to the dis-
carded Catherine of Aragon and her daughter to announce the
king's decision to divorce her, and secondly to place the crown

jewels in the hands of Queen Jane Grey, by order of the Duke of Northumberland. According to the Spanish Ambassador, Lady Jane was furious when William told her that her father-in-law, the Duke, intended to have his son crowned king.

When Queen Elizabeth came to visit him at Basing House she was so delighted with his hospitality that she playfully lamented his great age, 'for by my troth if my Lord Treasurer were but a young man I could find it in my heart to have him for a husband before any man in England'. He was created Earl of Wiltshire in 1531 and Marquess of Winchester the year after. At the age of eighty-seven he died in his own beautiful house and was buried in Basing church where so many of the Paulet family lie. He left no less than 107 descendants, of whom the most famous was John Paulet, 'Old Loyalty', the fifth Marquess of Winchester and premier Marquess of England.

He it was who held Basing House for the king in the Civil Wars, one of its most heroic episodes, with such skill and courage and against all Parliamentary odds until only Cromwell himself at last took it with 7,000 troops to help him. It is said the guards were playing cards when the final assault came and 'clubs are trumps as when Basing House was taken' is still a Hampshire saying. The Marquess's own brother, Lord Edward Paulet, had turned traitor. Though spared himself he was forced to act as hangman to the other conspirators.

There was no escape, no mercy; men fought to their death. Looting was rife and even the women were stripped naked and some of them raped; the soldiers were hanged. The total plunder was some quarter of a million pounds—'a good encouragement' said Cromwell before ordering the house to be burned to the ground.

The Marquess and his wife were sent to the Tower. The children were ordered to become Protestants. It was not until the Restoration that all his sequestered estates were returned to him and a recompense payment promised of £19,000, later reduced to £10,000. In final peace and quiet he lived out his life in the beautiful Englefield House near Reading in Berkshire, which he had acquired through marriage. He died in 1675 and was buried in Englefield church. John Dryden, then Poet Laureate, wrote his epitaph.

His son Charles was created Duke of Bolton, but the dukedom became extinct with the death of Harry, the sixth duke, in 1794, leaving no male issue. The Marquessate of Winchester and the minor honours devolved upon his kinsman George, twelfth Marquess of Winchester, a descendant of the second surviving son of the fourth marquess.

The titles of the present marquess, who is eighteenth in succession are Earl of Wiltshire and Baron St John of Basing.

PERCY

Earls of Northumberland

Arms: Quarterly; 1 and 4 or, a lion rampant azure; 2 and 3
gules, three luces hauriant argent.

Alnwick Castle, Northumberland, for some 700 years the home
and stronghold of the illustrious Percy family, is one of the
greatest of medieval English castles.

It stands on a small eminence above the river Aln, completely
dominating the town of Alnwick. Its massive towers, turrets and
curtain walls cover some five acres of ground, in the centre of
which stands the magnificent keep, built about 1350 by the first
earl. He also built the massive barbican guarding the main
entrance, having the famous Percy blue lion rampant and motto,
'Esperance', carved over the outer gateway.

This gateway has a superb Norman arch flanked by two
octagonal towers, but its huge doors are said to be Elizabethan.
High upon the barbican battlements and in strange contrast are
the eighteenth century carved figures of warriors repelling an

attack upon the castle. Beneath these figures are several shields bearing the coats of arms of many famous families allied to the house of Percy by marriage. The most prominent are those of Nevill, Bohun, de Clifford, Warenne, Plantagenet, FitzWalter, Umfraville and Arundel. In the very centre, between the flanking towers is the coat of arms of Edward III, France ancient and England quarterly.

In a narrow passage in the wall is the almost pitch dark prison. The iron staples in the wall where prisoners were chained when the dungeons were full may still be seen.

The three-storied battlemented Abbot's Tower was built about 1350 and was the residence of the Abbot of Alnwick when he was required at the castle. Somewhere between 1309 and 1315 the three-storied Constable's Tower was built, the only part of the castle open to visitors. It has not been altered since it was first erected.

By the middle of the eighteenth century scarcely anything remained of the original Norman castle, but it was then transformed into a vast palace by the Duke of Northumberland, and was again restored in the nineteenth century by the fourth duke.

In about 1450, very shortly before his death, the second earl built the Hotspur Tower. It was then part of the town of Alnwick whose encircling walls were almost twenty-one feet high, six feet thick, and a mile long. This grim and massive tower faces the visitor as he leaves the station at Alnwick and walks down Bondgate-Without, a reminder, if any was needed, of the former impregnability of the Percy strength.

The Percy tomb in Beverley Minster, Yorkshire, to the memory of Lady Eleanor, wife of the first lord, is considered to be one of the glories of medieval art, enriched as it is by carvings of angels, fruit, leaves, and symbolic beasts. An American tourist once broke off an angel as a souvenir, but twenty-eight years later it was found and returned to Beverley. Dugdale states that when the grave of this lady was opened in 1678, nearly 200 years after her death 'her body was found in a fair coffin of stone embalmed and covered with cloth of gold, and on her feet slippers embroidered with silke, and there was a wax lampe, a candle, and plate candle-sticke'. In the Percy chapel is the tomb of the fourth earl, murdered by the mob at Topcliffe. Under the clock is a helmet said to be that of Hotspur, and another near the flags is believed to have been that of the fifth earl, known as Percy the Magnificent.

The head of this great line was William de Percy, who came from the village of Percy-en-Auge in Calvados, Normandy. He had the additional name of *Alsgernons*, or 'William with the whiskers', whence many of his descendants have taken the name Algernon. He was a most distinguished military commander, and in return for his services in the Conquest, William the Conqueror granted him vast lands in Northumberland as tenant in chief and feudal lord of a barony of no less than thirty knights fee, being under tenant to Hugh, Earl of Chester.

The first of the many great family alliances, and certainly the most important, was when Agnes de Percy married Josceline of Louvain, brother of Queen Adela, second wife of Henry I. The enormous wealth of Agnes enabled her to insist upon him taking the name of Percy whilst replacing the ancient arms of the family, *azure five fusils conjoined fesswise or* by *or a lion rampant azure*, the arms of Brabant, from whose family her husband descended. There were several children of this marriage, the youngest of whom, Richard, was one of the twenty-five barons at the signing of Magna Carta by King John.

Henry de Percy, who bought the barony of Alnwick from Anthony Bek, Prince Bishop of Durham, was the first lord to be summoned to Parliament by Edward I.

Henry, the fourth lord, was a very distinguished military commander under Edward III, and was Marshal of England at the coronation of Richard II, who created him on that day the first Earl of Northumberland and a Knight of the Garter. He it was who made the second most important family alliance since it united with the equally powerful and illustrious family of Nevill, later Earls of Westmoreland, by marrying Margaret, daughter of Ralph, Lord Nevill of Raby. The son of this marriage was the renowned Hotspur.

The earl married secondly Maud, sister and co-heir of Anthony, Lord Lucy, who in return for settling the honours, vast lands, and castle of Cockermouth in Cumberland on the heirs of this marriage, demanded that his arms should be quartered with those of the house of Percy. Thus the Percy arms became *Quarterly; 1 and 4 or, a lion rampant azure; 2 and 3 gules, three luces hauriant argent.* A luce was a medieval pikefish and used as a play on the name Lucy.

The earl fought with distinction in the Scottish wars, capturing Berwick. A few years later the Scots, by bribing the governor, recaptured it. The Duke of Lancaster brought this to the notice of Parliament and the earl was sentenced to death, all his estates being forfeited. These were later restored to him by Henry IV, who in return for Percy's rebellion against, and dethronement of, Richard II, gave him the Isle of Man. In tenure of this he would carry, at the coronation of himself and all his successors, the sword which the king wore when he landed at Holderness.

Before long, however, Percy, as Warden of the Marches, made demands for lawful dues which he had not received. When the king refused, Percy at once put his son Hotspur at the head of his troops in open rebellion. Hotspur was slain at Shrewsbury and his father killed at Bramham, where he was met by Sir Thomas Rokeby, and fought a terrible battle in a blinding snowstorm. The earl's head, with its shining silver locks, was hacked from his body and sent to London, where it was stuck on a pike at London Bridge.

Hotspur, so named from his violent temper and rash courage, had been knighted by Richard II at his coronation. He was only thirteen, and a year later was fighting in the Scottish wars. He first bore the earlier Percy arms *Or, a lion rampant azure* with *a label of three points gules for difference.* On the death of his stepmother he quartered his arms with Lucy as his father had done but with a label.

Henry V restored all the attainted honours and titles of his father to Hotspur's eldest son, who had spent all his youth exiled in Scotland. He returned to England to receive his earldom, fought at Agincourt and was killed at St Albans in the first battle of the Wars of the Roses. Both his sons were later killed in battle.

Henry, third earl, married the daughter and sole heiress of Richard Poynings, who brought as her dowry the baronies of FitzPayn, Bryan, and Poynings, adding enormous wealth to an already immensely wealthy family. He died leading the van of the Lancastrians at Towton. Though attainted for treason his honours were restored to his eldest son Henry, fourth earl. He, when trying to levy taxes for the French wars for Henry VII, was murdered at Topcliffe, together with some of his attendants, by an angry mob. He lies buried in Beverley Minster.

Henry, fifth earl, died in peace though he fought in two battles. He left a Household Book and lived in great splendour with a lavish hospitality which earned him the local name of Percy the Magnificent. His second son was executed at Tyburn. His eldest son, Henry, sixth earl was even more prodigal and became known as Percy the Unthrifty, squandering his patrimony and estates wholesale. This may have been due to his father forcing him to marry Lady Mary Talbot when he was in love with Anne Boleyn. He lived and died a most unhappy man, grieving for his brother's execution, childless, living much alone and away from the world.

Henry, eighth earl, a staunch Catholic, plotted the ill-timed, rash, and fatal 'Rising in the North', which ended the Nevills of Raby line in ignominy and disgrace, and brought himself to the Tower. He was imprisoned for some time there and later found mysteriously murdered by three pistol shots from an unknown assailant.

Henry, ninth earl, was brought before the dreaded Star Chamber on a false charge of taking part in the Gunpowder Plot. He was fined £30,000, an enormous sum of money in those days, stripped of all his honours and titles, and sentenced to imprisonment for life in the Tower. His son, Algernon Percy, tenth earl, fought first against King Charles in the Civil War, and then supported the restoration of Charles II.

His son, Jocelyn Percy, eleventh earl, had a son and a daughter, the former predeceasing him, so that in 1670 the honours, save the baronies, of this great and historic family became extinct. His daughter, the Lady Elizabeth, who was twice married and twice widowed before she was sixteen, finally married Charles, Duke of Somerset, by whom she had thirteen children, her eldest son becoming seventh Duke of Somerset and first Earl of Northumberland of the new creation. There is, however, evidence that a junior male line existed until 1755, and may do still.

The present head of this very distinguished line is the Duke of Northumberland (Sir Hugh Algernon Percy), Earl of Northumberland, Earl Percy, Earl of Beverley, Baron Warkworth, of Warkworth Castle, and Lord Lovaine, Baron of Alnwick, Northumberland, and a Baronet.

The arms are: *Quarterly: 1st and 4th, grand quarters, 1st and 4th, counter-quartered, 1st and 4th, or, a lion rampant azure; 2nd and 3rd, gules, three luces hauriant argent,* for Lucy; *2nd and 3rd azure, five fusils conjoined in fesse or,* for Percy; *2nd and 3rd, grandquarters quarterly, 1st and 4th or, three bars wavy gules, 2nd and 3rd or, a lion's head erased within a double tressure flory counter-flory gules,* for Drummond.

There is a singular epilogue to this drama, for a certain James Percy, a trunk maker in Dublin, in 1670, the year of the eleventh earl's death, came to this country to claim all the honours, estates, and titles of the family.

For fifteen years he tenaciously fought his claim against the proud, rich, and powerful Duke of Somerset, being treated by Parliament as a criminal 'for daring to trouble the House of Lords about his claim'. He was defeated at all points, bringing his final action against a certain James Clark, who publicly declared Percy was an imposter. The verdict by the Lord Chief Justice was negative, for he stated: 'Percy had as much right to the Earldom of Northumberland as he, the Chief Justice, had to his coach and horses, which he had bought and paid for'.

This was followed by another action against John Wright, who had declared him illegitimate. Percy was awarded the verdict and damages of £300. Lawsuit after lawsuit followed, until finally the House of Lords declared his claim 'to be groundless, false and scandalous, and that he should be brought to West-minster Hall wearing a paper upon his breast on which were written the words "The false and impudent pretender to the Earldom of Northumberland" '.

It was the end of the trunk maker, though many there were who implicitly believed his claim, even more so when his son, Sir Algernon Percy, was elected, in 1699, Lord Mayor of Dublin.

POYNTZ

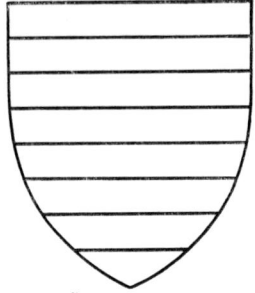

Arms: Barry of eight or and gules.

For over 300 years, from the fourteenth to the seventeenth century, members of the Poyntz family have been buried in their own private chapel of their own church which they built in the little village of Iron Acton, Gloucestershire, some ten miles from Bristol. Such was their munificence that even today a requiem mass is held there annually, a rare event indeed.

The church contains abundant evidence of their existence. In the choir lies the recumbent figure of a knight, almost certainly Sir John Poyntz who died in 1376. On the north side of the sanctuary is an armorial glass window containing the family coat of arms and one of their three crests. On the south side are the tomb and effigies of Sir Robert between his two wives, Ann and Catherine, the second having been murdered by their youngest son Maurice.

On the south side of the private chapel is a beautiful fifteenth-century canopied tomb with three coats of arms of the Acton family. On the eastern wall hang the helmet formerly borne on the dead lord's bier, a single spur, and a piece of leather surcoat belonging to the last Sir John, who died in 1680 after completing the ruin of the estates his father had begun. In the churchyard is the fine arched and canopied stone preaching cross, with eight shields, built by Sir Robert in 1439.

The head of the family came over with the Conqueror, and was granted vast lands in Herefordshire, Dorset, and Somerset. The first baron was created in 1295, the barony terminating with the death of the fourth baron, whose two daughters held it in abeyance, there being no male heir.

A younger branch of the line began with the first Sir John of Iron Acton, who was the son of Matilda, second wife of Sir Nicholas, second baron of the senior line. He was not only the ancestor of the Iron Acton line, which terminated in 1680, but also of the junior line of the Poyntzes of Midgham, Berkshire, and Cowdray Park and Battle Abbey in Sussex. This line terminated in 1840 with the death of the last male heir, William Stephen Poyntz.

Two other lines, however, later claimed descent. One was from Havant and Bedhampton in Northamptonshire, and another from Acton, County Armagh, in Ireland. A Sir Charles Poyntz, knighted in 1630, was father of Sir Toby Poyntz, MP, whose daughters and co-heiresses were Sarah, wife of Colonel Charles Stewart of Ballentoy, and Christian, wife of Roger Hall of Narrow Water, County Down. From the last name descends the family of Orr of Ballygowan. The former line took the original coat of arms, *barry of eight or and gules* but *within a bordure azure*. The latter reversed the tinctures but took the original crest, *a cubit arm erect, the fist clenched ppr, vested in a sleeve argent*.

Though successive members of the Iron Acton line took part in most of the military activities of those times, fighting for or against the king, or against the Scots, Welsh and French, they do not seem to have been outstanding militarily. All of them, however, held high offices under various sovereigns, receiving honours, knighthoods, and gifts, one of which was an annual tun of Gascony wine out of the ports of Southampton and Bristol given to Sir Anthony by Henry VIII.

For most of their time they seemed to be permanently in vendetta against the rich and powerful family of the Berkeleys of Berkeley Castle, today visited by thousands of people annually and where the family have lived for nearly 1,000 years. Smyth's *Lives of the Berkeleys*, one of the most detailed family histories ever written, fills page after page with details of their various feuds, lawsuits, and counter lawsuits over leases, fees simple, and once even suspected fraud. This was when Sir Nicholas Poyntz was accused of 'opening a sealed chest with the hot blade of a knife to extract a vital document about the rightful ownership of a manor'.

A serious attempt was made by both sides to end the feud and a marriage was arranged between Sir Nicholas Poyntz and Joan, daughter of Maurice the fifth Lord Berkeley, to take place on Midsummer Day, 1528, at Yate Court, quite near to Iron Acton and owned by Lord Berkeley. The marriage contract was an interesting one. Sir Nicholas's marriage portion was 600 marks 'whereof 100 at the wedding and 100 each year afterward'. A strange clause stated that if Sir Nicholas should pre-decease his bride-to-be before the wedding day she was to marry his brother Giles with the aforesaid dowry. Evidently the two families were now determined to end the war between them. The original marriage, however, was carried out and nine children were later born.

It was not long before the vendetta once again began, and Smyth was wearily writing in his great book, 'The riots and brawls have started again with a double chancery suit between my lord and Sir Nicholas Poyntz. Too often have these burst forth and blustered between these several posterities for five or more descents together. But I am unwilling to ravel one thread of that coat which among kindred should be seamless.'

After Sir Nicholas died his son carried on the fight, and by now Smyth was recording, 'the burning of ricks and havocking of deer in the parks'. Finally Poyntz, more impoverished than Berkeley by the constant and expensive litigation costs, did what he could to make some sort of peace. The last Sir Robert was almost completely ruined by lawsuits, mortgaging his property to the hilt. His son, Sir John, completed the final ruin of the family before he himself died in 1680. His death terminated the Iron Acton line and he was the last to be buried in the church.

The most important figure in the Midgham, Berkshire, line was Stephen Poyntz, 'the great light and ornament of his family'. He was a diplomat of considerable skill, ambassador to Sweden, and governor and household steward to the Duke of Cumberland, 'The Butcher of Culloden', who was the third son of George II.

In 1725 Poyntz bought the gracious mansion, Midgham House, still visible today from the Bath road between Newbury and Reading but now divided into flats. Though he claimed to have spent much money on the purchase some said it was a wedding present from the king when Poyntz married Anne Maria Mordaunt, who was a maid of honour to Queen Caroline, and a reigning beauty of her day, known as 'the Fair Circassian', because she had been so called in a poem.

Poyntz had considerable influence in Court circles, and a room over the main gateway of St James's Palace was known as Mr Poyntz's room. Walpole attacked him for spending so much public money on Swedish affairs, but he was widely respected for his kindliness and modesty, 'timorous to childishness' as a contemporary wrote. Carlyle, in his memoirs of Frederick the Great, trenchantly referred to Poyntz as 'a once bright gentleman now dim and obsolete'. Neither was his wife free from comment. With equal pungency Mrs Calderwood, the diarist, wrote of her towards the end of her life as 'a deaf, short-sighted, hackney-headed wife who played at cards from morning till night'. They both lie buried in Thatcham church in Berkshire.

His son inherited considerable estates in Berkshire and boasted 'that he could hunt from the Thames to the Kennet without asking anyone's permission'. Of his seven children Georgina Anne was painted by Romney. She married Sir Everard Falkener, who divorced her after fighting a duel in Hyde Park with her alleged lover, Lord John Townshend, who later married Georgina. Another daughter married the Earl of Cork.

The eldest son, William Stephen Poyntz, became MP for St Albans and acquired still more estates by marrying Elizabeth Mary Browne , daughter of the seventh Viscount Montagu of Cowdray Park.

They thus became heirs to the Cowdray curse, as related earlier; William Poyntz finally dying after six years of suffering following a hunting accident. Cowdray Park was sold outright for £300,000 even in its ruined state, and Midgham House for £84,000, very considerable sums of money in those days.

With his death the line terminated. Of the three surviving daughters and co-heiresses, Frances Helena became Lady Clinton; Elizabeth Georgina, Countess Spencer; and Isabella, Marchioness of Exeter.

TURBERVILLE

Arms: Ermine, a lion rampant gules crowned or.

Since the publication in 1891 of Thomas Hardy's novel *Tess of the d'Urbervilles* many thousands of people have made their pilgrimage to the beautiful parish church of Bere Regis ('Kingsbere'), ten miles from Dorchester in Dorset.

There, exactly as Hardy described it, is the south wall against which the waggon driver dumped the few poor worldly possessions of the Durbeyfields.

'Isn't your family vault your own freehold?' said Tess's mother, as she returned from a reconnoitre of the church and graveyard. 'Why of course 'tis, and that's where we will camp, girls, till the place of your ancestors finds us a roof.'

Tess then listlessly helps to put up the old four-poster bed.

Over the tester of the bedstead was a beautifully traceried window, of many lights, its date being the fifteenth century. It was called the d'Urberville Window, and in the upper part could be discerned heraldic emblems like those on Durbeyfield's old seal and spoon.

This splendid armorial window is a blaze of heraldic colour from twenty coats of arms, headed by the rampant red lion of the Turbervilles. After putting the children to bed Tess wanders round the churchyard before entering the church itself.

Within the window under which the bedstead stood were the tombs of the family, covering in their dates several centuries. They were canopied, altar-shaped, and plain; their carvings being defaced and broken; their brasses torn from the matrices, the rivet-holes remaining like martin-holes in a sand-cliff. Of all the reminders that she had ever received that her people were socially extinct there was none so forcible as this spoliation.

Though the Turbervilles have been immortalised in Hardy's novel under a similar name, they were a very real and important Norman family whose principal seat in Dorset was at Bere Regis, but who also owned vast lands in Devonshire, Berkshire, and Wales.

It was in 1242 when Bartholomew de Turberville was granted licence to build the private chapel or chantry at Bere Regis, where the great tombs are, 'for the use of himself, his household and guests, and his heirs to be served by a perpetual chaplain'. Their once splendid mansion to the east of the church, still known as Court Green was not finally demolished until 1832. There are bad portraits of some of them in an hotel near Wool and in the Dorset County Museum.

Their name came from the Normandy department of Eure where they lived before coming over to England with William the Conqueror. The earliest mention of them in history was in 1090, when Sir Payn Turbervill was one of twelve knights who fought for Jestin ap Gurgent, King of Glamorgan, against Rhese, Prince of South Wales, from which campaign he acquired considerable estates and the powerful Coyty Castle.

One of his descendants had a mansion at one time considered to be as splendid as that of Herbert, Earl of Pembroke. The cellars are mentioned as being overstocked with the choicest wines he personally imported from Brussels, Bordeaux and Sicily.

At an early date the family acquired possession of Ewenny Priory in Glamorgan, now in ruins but open to the public. This branch of the family has always omitted the final 'e' from the name and does so down to this day.

At Cadeleigh, 4½ miles from Tiverton, Devon, is a costly and splendid tomb to Sir Simon Leach and his wife Katherine, who was a daughter of Nicholas Turbervill of Crediton.

Yet another branch of the family settled at East Hendred in Berkshire as early as 1166, and in 1248 Geoffrey de Turberville sold land to Poughley Priory; the document of sale is recorded in the muniments of Westminster Abbey. In 1265 John de Turberville founded a chapel within his manor of Arches.

The first recorded dates of their existence in Dorset were in 1204 and 1208, when Henry de Turberville was engaged in lawsuits concerning his property in Melcombe, Walter de Turberville having had all his lands forfeited for his allegiance to the barons against the king.

The first of the three important members of the family to make their name in English history was Henry, son of Robert. Throughout almost the whole of King John's troubled reign he had been loyal to him and was known to be not only a soldier of distinction but a naval commander as well. In the last year of his reign John rewarded his loyal subject with many estates in Devon and Dorset which had been forfeited to the crown. De Turberville continued to serve Henry III with the same loyal allegiance, helping Hubert de Burgh to defeat the French fleet under Eustace the Monk in the Straits of Dover. For his services he received still more estates in Wiltshire, Suffolk, Lincolnshire and Bedfordshire, and was appointed to the very high office of Seneschal of Gascony.

During the five difficult years of office in France his letters to the king reveal a serious lack of money to help him conduct his campaigns to deal with a conspiracy in Bordeaux, a rebellion in Bayonne, and unsettled relations with the French king himself. Failing to get the required money he begged the king to relieve him of his governorship. Henry refused, saying he must hold the office until he himself came to Gascony to investigate his troubles.

Finally, in 1233, he was recalled and sent to Wales to deal with the revolt of Marshal, Earl of Pembroke, whose castle at Carmarthen was held by the Welsh rebels who had risen to support him against the king.

Turberville went immediately to Bristol, embarked a force of soldiers, and sailed up the Towy to the castle and town of Carmarthen. The bridge over the river and immediately below the castle was held by the rebels; Turberville wasted no time on naval manoeuvres but simply rammed it. The defenders who were not captured were drowned. The castle was stormed and taken. A year later he was reappointed Seneschal of Gascony and returned to France. From there he was sent to fight the Lombards. His life for the next seven years was one military campaign after another. His last decision was to join the crusade headed by Richard of Cornwall, but his death in the year 1239 prevented this.

His wife, Hawise, had all his Devonshire estates assigned to her. His illegitimate daughter Edelina, who had married Elie de Blenac, a Santongeais, received all her father's Bordeaux estates, and grants of money were settled on her. His sister, Lucy, who had married into the Bingham family, later earls of Lucan, inherited the estates of Melcombe.

The gatehouse of the manor of Melcombe Bingham, built 700 years ago with walls 9ft thick, was the original home of the Binghams. The house, with its carved pinnacles, armorial glass windows, and Tudor and Queen Anne wings still stands today.

Sir Henry de Turberville's great-grandson, Sir Robert of Bere and Anderton, was involved in a complaint lodged by the Abbess of Tarrant Kaines. She alleged that he, 'a chevalier together with many others had transgressed her right of free warren at Bere, hunted and fished her preserves, felled her trees and assaulted her servants'. A special commission was appointed to investigate the case. Sir Robert died in 1424.

In 1497 Dorset supported the rebellion of Perkin Warbeck, who, by claiming to be one of the two young princes supposed to have been murdered in the Tower by Richard III, spuriously pretended to the throne. The Yorkists promptly and eagerly took up his cause against Henry VII, together with the monasteries, who generally favoured the commoners.

There was a second rising by the people of Dorset when Warbeck invaded south-west England and besieged Exeter, before being captured, sent to the Tower, and executed at Tyburn. Though the king gave a general pardon to all the rebels he imposed on them very heavy fines, the collection of which was carried out with much extortion and injustice, the complaints being brought before Sir John Turberville.

A few years later Sir John with other great nobles accompanied Catherine of Aragon on her bridal progress from Sherborne to Shaftesbury, the Dorset stage of her long journey across England. He married Isabella, daughter of John Cheverell, and was succeeded by his son James, the second of the three great figures in the Turberville family, who was born at Bere Regis, was a staunch Roman Catholic, as were all his ancestors, and was later appointed Bishop of Exeter by Queen Mary.

When Elizabeth came to the throne, however, he very soon came into conflict with her over her anti-papal doctrines, and was sharply critical of the persecutions and tortures she had ruthlessly carried out, finally refusing to take the oath of supremacy.

He was immediately deprived of his bishopric, and after joining other similarly punished prelates in a letter of remonstrance to the obdurate queen, was sent to the Tower. He was later released and placed in the custody of the Bishop of London. Much later still he was liberated on production of sureties for his good behaviour, living the rest of his life in retirement and liberty. 'This Bishop Turberville', wrote Fuller in his *Worthies of England*, 'carries something of trouble in his name though nothing but mildness and meekness in his nature, the privacy of whose life caused the obscurity of his death.'

The third outstanding family figure was George Turberville, born in 1540 at Winterbourne Whitchurch. He had none of the singular qualities of his ancestors but became instead an Elizabethan poet of no little merit. Three of his poems are published in the *Oxford Book of 16th century verse*. They are 'The Lover to his Lady' and 'The Lover to the Thames of London, to favour his Lady Passing thereon' from *Epitaphs, Epigrams, Songs and Sonnets*. And from *Tragical Tales* a poem 'To his Friend, Promising that though her Beauty Fade yet his Love will Last'.

His fine scholarship at Winchester College when he was only fourteen came to the knowledge of Thomas Randolph, who, on his appointment as ambassador to the Empress of Russia took Turberville with him as his secretary to act on behalf of English merchants trading in that country. Turberville was very soon writing home of his experiences in Russia, many of his letters being in verse, describing the natives as 'people passing rude to vices vile inclined'. Some of his descriptions of the country are in *Hakluyt's Voyages*.

It is recorded that on his return to England he was much sought after by people who found him 'a most accomplished gentleman'. His duties as secretary to Randolph must in themselves have been often difficult, for his master was all too much involved in manipulations between Elizabeth and Scotland over the marriage of Mary, Queen of Scots, as well as making frequent missions abroad.

If, as has been said, the Bere Regis line became extinct when two old ladies died at Putney in 1780, the name is still to be found in Dorset. The Welsh line is extant through marriage inheritances, the name and arms of Turbervill being assumed by Royal Licence, first in 1797 and again in 1867.

In spite of the historical truth of the existence of this ancient family, however, the majority of the countless pilgrims to Dorset come to find *Tess of the d'Urbervilles*. The unhappy and immortal story of the dairymaid is known all over the world, and the real family, on which Hardy based his great novel, sleep undisturbed in their great vaults under their own red rampant lion of Turberville they so proudly bore when they lived.

CAMPBELL

Dukes of Argyll

Arms: Quarterly; 1 and 4 gyronny of eight or and sable, for Campbell; 2 and 3 argent, a galley (or lymphad) sable, sails furled flag and pennants flying and oars in action ppr, for the Lordship of Lorne.

The great Scottish castle of Inverary in Argyllshire, home of the dukes of Argyll for over two centuries, attracts many thousands of tourists annually from all over the world.

It is built of blue-grey chlorite slate and stands on the edge of Loch Fyne, amidst immense parklands and trees, its four flanking turreted towers giving it an almost feudal look. Its interior is even more impressive, and most especially the splendid ceiling of the Armoury Hall, covered with the coats of arms of the great Campbell clan of which each successive duke is the hereditary chief.

Their history has been one long series of striking successes, doubtless due to a natural inheritance of shrewdness, calculated cunning, ruthlessness, high personal courage, indomitable energy, and considerable aggression. These qualities, together with brilliant marriage alliances, have probably brought them more wealth, lands, titles and honours than any other Scottish clan. Two of them were also created English peers, and one of these buried in Westminster Abbey with an epitaph by Alexander Pope.

The present castle was first erected by the third duke in 1743, on the strong advice of his wife, the Dowager Duchess of Hamilton, replacing the old family home built in 1457 by Colin, the first earl. Before all this, however, was the original and impregnable stronghold of the Campbells, the castle of Inchconnell on the southern tip of Loch Awe, probably eleventh century, and now a ruin.

As with so many Scottish families the origin of the clan of Campbell is almost legendary, but the first recorded appearance of them was in 1266 when Gillespic received a royal charter of lands in Clackmannan. One of his descendants, another Gillespic who married the rich heiress of Lochaw, received a further royal charter.

All the authorities agree, however, that the first great figure to emerge was Sir Colin or Mac Cailein Mor (Great), a title used to this very day by the head of the house of Campbell. He was a distinguished soldier who gave devoted service to Robert the Bruce, was killed in a fight with the rival MacDougall clan, and buried at Kilchrennan in 1294.

It was his son, Sir Neil, who gave the clan its first great rise to power and wealth when he married, as his second wife, Lady Mary, sister of Robert the Bruce. Indeed, it is true to say that the constant loyalty of the Campbells to the Bruce, both in victory and defeat, was the foundation of all their future greatness. After the battle of Bannockburn their eldest son John not only received as a reward all the lands of the defeated Earl of Atholl, but the earldom as well. As he had no male issue, however, the title soon became extinct.

Sir Neil's great-great-grandson Sir Duncan was created first Lord Campbell by James II of Scotland in 1445, and under his leadership the clan acquired its unquestioned supremacy in the

Hebrides and Argyllshire over the fast-waning power of the MacDougalls, whose vast lands had become forfeited and given to the Campbells.

His grandson Colin, was created first Earl of Argyll in 1457. Thereafter the earldom lasted 244 years before it became a dukedom, no less than ten earls succeeding to the title. Colin made a most distinguished marriage with the eldest daughter of John, Lord Lorne, thereby putting an end to the bitter and bloody feuds which had existed between them for over 250 years. To seal the alliance heraldically the Campbells quartered their own arms with the Galley of Lorne, the ancient badge of the clan. The title of Lord Lorne, later Marquess of Lorne, is borne by the heir apparent to the dukedom of Argyll down to the present day.

Archibald, second earl, who was killed at Flodden, had several daughters, one of whom, Elizabeth, married the ferocious Lachlan Cattanach Maclean, eleventh chief of his clan. Their dislike of each other was rapid and mutual, for reasons that are given in the chapter on Maclean of Duart (p 153).

He had her rowed out to a small sea-beaten rock between Lismore and Mull, still known as 'Lady's Rock', to be drowned by the high tide. She was fortunately seen by two of her kinsmen in a passing boat, rescued and hidden whilst her husband went through a mock funeral before leaving for Edinburgh, where he was promptly murdered by his brother-in-law as a revenge.

Archibald, fourth earl, was one of the first Scottish nobles to turn Protestant, which resulted in the Campbells working more than any other family for the final triumph of this religion over Papacy in Scotland. His son John, who succeeded him, was even more zealous. He made a distinguished marriage with a natural daughter of James V; she was therefore a half-sister of Mary, Queen of Scots. But the repeated quarrels and final separation of the earl and countess gave great offence to the Protestant cause. The earl became deeply involved in the plot to murder Darnley and to arrange a marriage between the queen and Bothwell.

Archibald, seventh earl, known as 'the Grim' by the Highlanders, became the principal character in another astonishing drama. In 1592 Campbell of Calder, one of the young earl's guardians was shot dead in his house; a few days later 'the bonnie Earl' was murdered by Huntly. Archibald was to die next by poison but the plot failed. When Archibald later learned the full extent of their designs and two men had been hanged, his revenge was swift and terrible. He declared a war of total extermination of Huntly and all his clan for murdering 'the bonnie Earl', during which unspeakable atrocities were committed on both sides, and the northern lands laid to utter waste by a scorched earth policy carried out without mercy or pity. The bloodshed was only finally ended by the defeated Huntly fleeing to Denmark, and Campbell of Glenorchy being imprisoned in Edinburgh for his support of him.

It was eight years before James VI of Scotland, just before his accession as James I to the English throne, forced a reconciliation between the two chieftains, and this by a betrothal of Huntly's eldest son to Argyll's eldest daughter. In addition the two earls were authorised to continue the warfare they both delighted in by wiping out the Macgregors, which they did so thoroughly that they became virtually extinct.

Archibald, the celebrated eighth earl, was elevated as first Marquess of Argyll, bringing the house of Campbell to a political power higher than ever before in its history. He was undoubtedly the most influential Scottish noble in the land between the years 1640 and 1650. When Montrose raised his standard for Charles I in Scotland the Marquess marched at the head of 500 men, but was so defeated and his lands so devastated 'that not a four-footed beast in the whole county was left'. His ruin was such that the Government had to grant him money to support his family.

He secured one valuable concession, however, and that was a ratified contract from Charles I to try and bring to the surface the Armada treasure ship *Florencion*, blown up by one of the clan Maclean in Tobermory Bay, Isle of Mull, where it had sought provisions, and said to have contained £30,000,000. Both his son and grandson renewed these contracts but the ship and its treasure still lie where they first went down.

After the execution of Charles I, when Prince Charles was crowned King of Scotland, the Marquess himself placed the crown upon his head. When Cromwell conquered Scotland the Marquess was driven into retreat at Inverary Castle, where he managed to hold out for a year before being suddenly invaded by sea. Though he came to uneasy terms with Cromwell, his son joined the Royalist party.

In 1641, during the Wars of Montrose the Argylls, on the opposite side to their implacable enemies, the Clan Maclean of Duart, treacherously offered to take over the Maclean debts to the crown, some £30,000 in Scots pounds. As the years passed this reached the astronomical figure of £120,000 and the Macleans were on the verge of ruin. The Argyll Synod pitilessly foreclosed, taking in payment all their lands in Morvern, Tiree, and Mull, and even for a time, until it was restored to them, the family home and stronghold of Duart Castle in Mull.

At the Restoration the Marquess went to London to offer his allegiance, but his many enemies and the treachery of General Monk, caused his immediate arrest and expulsion to Edinburgh. He was tried and sentenced to death for treacherous compliance with Cromwell's usurpation, and beheaded at Edinburgh Cross by 'The Maiden', an instrument resembling the guillotine, and his head stuck on the west end of the Tolbooth where Montrose's head had been earlier.

His son Archibald later shared the same fate, but escaped from his first sentence of death for treachery by a clever ruse of his step-daughter, Lady Sophia Lindsay, who disguised him as her page and helped him to reach Holland, where he became involved in a plot with the Duke of Monmouth to vindicate the rights and liberties of both England and Scotland following the death of Charles II, which led them both to the scaffold. Argyll was captured, sent to Edinburgh with every kind of indignity put on him during his journey, refused a fresh trial, put in irons, and finally executed in the same brutal manner as his father, his head also being stuck on the Tolbooth.

His eldest son, the tenth earl, after first taking refuge in

Holland, accompanied the Prince of Orange to England in 1688. He was created first Duke of Argyll. Macaulay is particularly virulent about him describing him as 'the descendant of eminent men and the parent of eminent men, but he was unworthy both of his ancestry and of his progeny and noted for little else but his polished manner and a spendthrift style of living'. He married a daughter of the notorious Duke of Lauderdale, living with her so unhappily that he took a mistress and set up house with her near Newcastle. His death, according to one historian 'was miserable and discreditable'.

His son, the second duke, was totally different, being a man of outstanding courage and ability. He was a colonel at seventeen and one of Marlborough's best generals at Blenheim, Ramillies, and Oudenarde, for which he was handsomely rewarded by being created Baron Chatham and Earl, later Duke, of Greenwich in the English peerage. He was buried with great honour in Westminster Abbey with a huge and elaborate monument, and a laudatory epitaph by Pope:

> Argyll, the State's whole thunder born to wield
> And shake alike the senate and the field.

Though twice married he had no male issue so that all his English titles became extinct, but his brother Archibald succeeded as third Duke of Argyll.

He it was who built the new castle of Inverary. He also formed from six independent companies of local militia the famous Black Watch regiment, so named because of the contrast between their dark tartan uniform and the bright red coats of the regular army.

The fourth duke, a shrewd and kindly man, was a grandson of the ninth earl who was beheaded, and both he and his son, later the fifth duke, played a large part in the Forty Five rebellion, raising levies, organising supplies, and fighting at Culloden. He married a famous beauty, Mary, daughter of Lord Bellendon.

John succeeded his father as fifth duke and he married an even more famous beauty, Elizabeth, Dowager Duchess of Hamilton, formerly one of the two celebrated Gunning sisters, under whose advice he completed the building of the present castle. Her late husband, the sixth Duke of Hamilton, had married her in great haste at night, in such a rush that he actually forgot the ring and substituted a bed-curtain ring which was found for him. Lord Coventry, in equal haste, married her sister.

Dr Johnson and Boswell visited them here, but whilst the duchess liked the doctor she snubbed Boswell 'because of his great impudence'. At the time of her death the duchess had become the mother of no less than four men destined to become dukes, two of Argyll and two of Hamilton. She was also created an English peeress as Baroness Hamilton of Hambledon, Co Leicester.

John, the ninth duke made an even more splendid marriage with the Princess Louise, a daughter of Queen Victoria. He was also a great personal friend of Carlyle, Tennyson, and Macaulay, and was made Governor General of Canada.

The Campbell clan exists today under its chieftain Mac Cailein Mor because of its early allegiance to Robert the Bruce and subsequent loyalty to every reigning sovereign. Its immense power stemmed from an outstanding insight and ability to weigh up any situation which would prove advantageous, and to exploit that advantage to the limit at every point in its long, troublesome, and always stormy history.

HAMILTON

Dukes of Hamilton & Brandon

Arms: Quarterly; I and IV grandquarters, quarterly 1 and 4, gules, three cinquefoils ermine for Hamilton; 2 and 3, argent, a lymphad sable with the sails furled ppr flagged gules for Arran; II and III grandquarters, argent, a man's heart gules ensigned with an imperial crown ppr, on a chief azure three stars of the first for Douglas. His Grace places in the centre of his shield the escutcheon of Chatelherault, viz. azure, three fleurs-de-lis or.

The thirteenth-century Brodick Castle in the Isle of Arran now the property of the Scottish National Trust, was for nearly 500 years the home of the Hamiltons, and earlier still it was a strategic viking fortress. This splendid red sandstone castle dominates the Bay of Brodick, is set amidst some of the most beautiful scenery in Scotland, and visited annually by some 40,000 people.

Here, in 1306, Robert the Bruce prepared for his invasion of Scotland, his room still one of the treasures of the castle as well as the magnificent drawing room ceiling covered with coats of arms, and the beautiful gardens.

The Hamiltons are a most illustrious family, first of all the peerage of Scotland after the Crown, and in addition to Brodick Castle they had the ancient barony of Cadzow with its castle overhanging the Clyde, Craignethan Castle, and Hamilton Palace. This last, demolished by coal mining, still preserves the hunting lodge of Chatelherault in the High Parks of the former building.

The family is supposed to have derived its name from the ancient Leicestershire manor of Hambledon in England, granted to their ancestor Bellomont, whom William the Conqueror created Earl of Leicester.

In the reign of Edward II, Walter de Hamilton, as the result of a quarrel with the king's favourite in which the latter was killed, was forced to flee with his servant across the border into Scotland. Here they changed clothes with two woodcutters and, taking their places, were overtaken by their pursuers. Hamilton, fearing his servant's anxiety might betray them, started at once to saw through a tree, crying out the word 'Through', which the pursuers mistook for a direction ahead and galloped off. Since that day the Hamilton crest has been a saw cutting through a tree, and their motto 'Through'.

Robert the Bruce, who welcomed Hamilton, granted him the ancient barony and castle of Cadzow and the title of Lord Hamilton of Cadzow. It was this early allegiance to the Bruce and later loyalty to the Stuarts which brought equal wealth and misfortune to the Hamiltons. The proximity of their estates to the powerful Douglas family gave them a kinsmanship which at first ended disastrously but later revived by intermarriage.

In 1450 Hamilton and Douglas went to Rome and Canterbury, and were shortly afterwards in revolt against James III. The tyranny and anarchy of the Black Douglases was equalled only by that of the barons in King Stephen's reign. Their lawlessness ended with the murder of two of them in Edinburgh Castle, one by the king himself. They were utterly defeated at Arkenholme in 1455, and their power, if not ended, at least checked. Their defeat was largely due to defection by Hamilton, who advised Douglas to postpone his attack. 'If you are afraid or tired', answered the arrogant tyrant, 'you may depart when you please'. Stung by this retort Hamilton deserted, not without previous bribery from the king for so doing, and was rewarded by the vast Douglas estates. He then married Princess Mary, the king's sister, through whom his descendants became next heirs to the crown after the Stuarts. Besides his legitimate offspring he had many bastards.

His eldest son, Sir James, who succeeded him, was created Earl of Arran and granted the island of that name which still belongs to the family. He was cruel and had a vicious temper which soon led him into another bloody feud with Douglas, now the Earl of Angus, in which, together with their retinues, they fought hand to hand in the High Street of Edinburgh in a fracas known as 'Clear the Causeway'. Hamilton was badly defeated and seventy men were killed before he and his bastard son made their escape by seizing a coal-horse, discarding its load, and riding off.

He was succeeded by his legitimate son James, who, according to a contemporary historian, 'was weak, foolish, in every way a poor creature blown about by every wind of feeling and public opinion, everything by turn and nothing long'. He became a Catholic, renounced England for France and received, as an award for his effort to match the Dauphin with the young Queen of Scots, the dukedom of Chatelherault.

After the abdication of Mary, Queen of Scots, he attempted control of Scotland and was imprisoned for a time by the Regent, the Earl of Moray, in Edinburgh Castle. The Regent was later murdered by a member of the Hamilton family who was afterwards hanged for his crime from the Bridge of Stirling. For three years after this Scotland was torn by anarchy and bloodshed organised by the Hamiltons in their attempts to reach the throne.

James, who succeeded, became insane, so that his brother John took the title. The youngest of the three sons, Lord Claud Hamilton, was created first Baron Paisley, and his son James was created first Earl of Abercorn.

The Lord John Hamilton who succeeded his insane brother

was at one time a candidate for the hand of Queen Mary, and so deeply committed himself in her cause that he was attainted, driven into exile, and all his estates and titles confiscated. It might well have been the extinction of the Hamilton line of nobility had not King James restored everything to him, even raising him to be Marquess of Hamilton. He had a number of illegitimate as well as legitimate children, in accordance with the accepted custom of those times.

His son James, who succeeded him, was created Earl of Cambridge, a title borne only by the English royal family. He died very suddenly at Whitehall and was suspected of being poisoned by the loathed Duke of Buckingham, himself shortly afterwards assassinated by Felton.

James, third marquess, called by Clarendon 'that man of compromise', was astute enough to be created Marquess of Clydesdale, Lord Aven and Innerdale, and first Duke of Hamilton. He was granted £10,000 to levy troops for Sweden against Germany, and in his absence Lord Reay brought a charge that being next heir to the Scottish throne Hamilton would use those levied troops to support his claim; a charge which, though refuted, stuck to him for the rest of his life.

His influence with Charles I was so great that he actually slept in the king's bedroom. When, however, he joined him at Oxford the court forced the king to yield him up. He was arrested, sent first to Pendennis Castle and then to St Michael's Mount in Cornwall, was liberated by the Parliamentary General Fairfax, and after being soundly beaten with the Scottish army at Preston he was tried as Earl of Cambridge and an English subject, and beheaded in 1649. Two years later his brother was killed at the battle of Worcester.

As neither left male issue the dukedom reverted to the duke's niece Anne, third Duchess of Hamilton, who finally brought the two powerful families of Hamilton and Douglas together by marrying Lord William Douglas, Earl of Selkirk. In 1663 they were created Duke and Duchess of Hamilton, the earldom of Selkirk being transferred to their second son.

James succeeded as fourth duke and was later created Duke of Brandon. Parliament took strong exception to this, declaring that no Scottish peer created an English peer since the Union could take his seat in the House of Lords, and this decision was not rescinded until the eighth Duke of Hamilton was permitted to sit there as fifth Duke of Brandon. A further storm blew up when he received the Order of the Garter, having already the Order of the Thistle, an unprecedented double honour. His character has been brilliantly portrayed in Thackeray's *Henry Esmond*, but Mackay was much less flattering. 'He had a coarse, black complexion, fickleness, bravery, rough manners, ambition, was haughty and was a violent enemy.'

Like his predecessors he was loyal to the sovereign, and the Jacobites hoped he might once again bring back the Stuarts, especially when he was appointed ambassador extraordinary to France. Before he even set out, however, he was killed in a duel with the notoriously evil Lord Mohun, instigated, it was said, by the Whigs. The duel took place at dawn in Hyde Park. Even when both fell 'they fought like enraged lions' according to Mohun's second, General Macartney, who finally killed the duke, fled to the continent, and later surrendered himself. He was tried for murder, acquitted, and sentenced for homicide.

James, sixth duke, made a spectacular marriage with Elizabeth, one of the 'two Gunning sisters', the most celebrated beauties of their day. He was in such haste to marry her that in the midnight ceremony he forgot the ring and had to substitute a curtain-pole ring which was found in the church. Both he and the duchess loved Brodick Castle and did much to improve and beautify it. He also had the hunting lodge of Chatelherault built in the High Parks of Hamilton Palace. The duchess intensely disliked and snubbed Boswell when he and Dr Johnson were guests in the castle. After the duke's death she married the Duke of Argyll and became the mother of four dukes, two Hamiltons and two Argylls. She was also created a peeress of Great Britain in her own right as Baroness of Hamilton of Hambledon, Co Leicester, the original county home of the family nearly 800 years previously.

Alexander, tenth duke, was noted for his fine taste in the arts and improved Brodick Castle even more than the sixth duke. He married the youngest daughter of that great English eccentric William Beckford of Fonthill Abbey, who wrote *Vathek*. Many of his ivory and porcelain figures may still be seen in the castle.

William, eleventh duke, married in 1845 Princess Marie of Baden, cousin-german of the French Emperor Napoleon III from whom he requested and received confirmation of his title Duke of Chatelherault, previously granted to his ancestor the second Earl of Arran in 1546. This title was also claimed by the Marquess of Abercorn, whose line is still extant, because in 1651 the Abercorn line became male representative of the house of Hamilton. Since the ducal line continued to bear the name and inherited the chieftainship, the arms of Abercorn in Scotland have never been allowed the Hamilton arms without a label for cadency.

William, twelfth duke, seems to have made every possible effort to squander and dissipate the vast family estates and fortune in an unchecked social round of pleasure, hardly ever visiting the island of Arran. As the result of a bucolic lawsuit against his agent it was disclosed that his liabilities were some £1,250,000, an astronomical sum of money in those days. There was a forced sale of a magnificent collection of books, pictures and china, together with the famous Beckford library, to pay off some of the debt, the sale lasting forty days.

His sister, Lady Mary Victoria, married the eldest son of the reigning Prince of Monaco. After bearing him a son she left him and applied to Rome for a dissolution of her marriage under special dispensation. Her plea was that she had been forced by her parents into the marriage, had never loved him, and even during the marriage ceremony kept saying to herself: 'I will not marry him. He shall not be my husband'. The Papal Court decreed the marriage null and void, and she straightaway married a Hungarian nobleman.

As the duke died with no male heir he was succeeded by his kinsman Alfred Douglas, styled Sir Douglas Douglas-Hamilton. Amongst the many titles and high offices the dukes of Hamilton have held are those of Premier Peer of Scotland, Heir Male of the House of Douglas, Hereditary Keeper of Holyrood House, and claimants to the dukedom of Chatelherault, the last supported by the superimposition of the escutcheon of Chatelherault over the quartered Hamilton arms.

MACDONALD

Barons Macdonald of Macdonald

Arms: Quarterly; 1, argent, a lion rampant gules, armed
and langued azure; 2, or, a hand in armour fessways holding
a cross-crosslet fitchee gules; 3, or, a lymphad sails furled
and oars in action sable flagged gules; 4, vert, a salmon
naiant in fess ppr; over all on an inescutcheon *en surtout or*
an eagle displayed gules, surmounted of a lymphad sails
furled oars in action sable.

The great nineteenth-century stone castle of Armadale, seat of the
Macdonalds, Lords of the Isles, stands in the far south of the
Scottish island of Skye. Once there was an earlier castle where Dr
Johnson and Boswell were frigidly received by the lord of those
days, and long before that the two great clan strongholds of
Dunscaith and Duntulm, now in ruins.

High up on the wall of Armadale Castle, beyond the twin
turreted entrance, is the huge stained glass window depicting the
figure of Somerled Macdonald, in his yellow Gaelic robe, with

his shield, long battle axe, and the two proudly defiant words *Rex Insularum* or Lord of the Isles.

He it was who first emerged clearly from the dark legends of the origin of his clan, the oldest, most numerous and most powerful of all the Scottish clans. They claim their original descent as far back as AD 125, when Conn of the Hundred Battles, High King of Ireland reigned.

Somerled was born of a Celtic father and Norwegian mother, hence his Norse name. He married Ragnhild, daughter of Olaf, King of Man. His advance to power was rapid and formidable, so much so that when Malcolm IV called upon him to relinquish his possessions, for he now proclaimed himself Regulus of Argyll, King of Man, and Lord of the Isles, Somerled actually declared war on Malcolm and sailed against him at the head of 160 galleys.

He was assassinated by his nephew in a most cruel manner and died in 1164, leaving his son Reginald as his successor, though there were several sons, legitimate and bastards. This led to considerable confusion in the division of his vast lands and to the foundation of the very many cadet lines such as the MacAlisters, MacIan of Ardnamurchan, Macdonalds of Glencoe, Clan Ranald, Macdonalds of Keppoch, Sleate and Loch Aish, to name only a few.

Whatever disputes arose between them, and they were many and bitter, the clans united to a man against a common enemy, and they played a very considerable part indeed in the final overthrow of the Norse power in Scotland and the revival of the inherent and traditional Gaelic influence.

The real Lordship of the Isles began in 1354 and ended with its forfeiture in 1493 under four great Macdonald lords, John, Donald, Alexander, and a second John. They had enormous power not only over all the western isles but whole areas of Scotland itself, over-running the mainland and capturing Inverness no less than seven times. They acquired either through marriage or loot the earldom of Ross (ancestors of the earls of Antrim, Wardens of the Marches), and the two powerful Skye castles of Dunscaith and Duntulm. They were in constant and bloody feuds with the Macleans, the MacLeods, and the fiercely hated Campbells. Their loyalty and obedience to their chief was total and absolute. They had their own bards, pipers, doctors, purse and sword bearers, and musicians. When James IV alarmed at their massive power was finally compelled to offer them crown charters for their lands and allegiance to sovereignty, they finally submitted to forfeiture with singular goodwill, though there were two more rebellions after this.

These were led by Donald Dubh, son of Angus Og, legitimated son of the last lord. Donald's first attempt ended in his imprisonment, and Donald Gorm of the house of Sleate, next in succession, continued the revolt. This also failed when he was killed trying to capture the Mackenzie stronghold, Eilean Donan Castle. He was wounded in the foot by a barbed arrow severing an artery from which he shortly died.

Donald Dubh escaped from prison and immediately made his second attempt to defy the king, sailing against him with a force of 4,000 men and 160 galleys, supported in his attempt by Henry VIII of England, but he died during the revolt and this attempt to overthrow sovereignty finally collapsed.

The clan remained without a chief for almost 200 years. The septs and vassals of the powerful sovereign lordship were divided into some nine independent clans. In 1660 Charles II restored the ancient name and chiefship to Aeneas Macdonald of Glengarry, as Lord Macdonald and Aros, but this was limited to the heirs male of his body.

This expired in 1680 and it was then that the important cadet line of the house of Sleate merged into the senior line as Sir James Macdonald of Sleate, Bart, Chief of the Clan Huistean, was received by Parliament as his heir. The first baronet had been created by Charles I with precedence above all others except one, in recognition of his great services to the Stuarts.

Thus the whole pattern of life in the Highlands changed, for where before the traditional obedience and allegiance to a chief was total and absolute, this was now given with the same loyalty to the sovereign power, always before refuted and defied. The

Macdonalds were some of the finest supporters of the Stuarts, even after their cause had become forever lost.

The heir of Sir James, Sir Alexander Macdonald of Macdonald, seventh baronet, had the chiefship restored in his person by erection of all the Sleate estates into the feudal barony of Macdonald, and in 1776 his son was created first Lord Macdonald.

Under an Act of Parliament of 1847 all their estates in Skye, together with the 'fairy castle' of Dunscaith, descended to Alexander Godfrey, seventh Lord Macdonald, who had been officially recognised by Lyon Court as Macdonald of Macdonald, chief of the name, and received restoration of the undifferenced arms of the ancient Macdonald chiefs. The later title 'of the Isles' which the Macdonalds of Sleate added has never been officially recognised by Lyon Court.

Due to the marriage of the first Baron Macdonald to Elizabeth Bosville, the Yorkshire estates of her father came into the family, their son taking the name of Bosville. The Macdonalds of Sleate lived for some years on their property at Thorpe Hall, near Driffield, Yorkshire, and some lie buried in Rudston church, far away indeed from their beloved western isles. Sir Alexander, fourteenth baronet, died in 1933. He was organist and choirmaster at the church and is commemorated in a stained glass window seated at the organ he gave and surrounded by choristers.

Of the other numerous clans the most important were those of Glencoe and Glengarry. The Macdonalds of Glencoe were cruelly massacred in 1692 by the Argyll regiment, who swept on them at dawn whilst they slept, murdering men, women and even children in cold blood, practically exterminating the clan.

The Glengarry clan descend from the Clan Ranald line through Donald, a younger son of the founder Ranald. They were extremely loyal to the Stuarts, who created one of them Lord Macdonald and Aros, eighth feudal Baron of Glengarry, and chief of the name clan of Macdonald. As he had no male heir, however, the title lapsed with the succession of his nephew.

It would be impossible to set out in detail the events in the picturesquely histrionic life of its last great chief, Colonel Alastair

Ranaldson Macdonald, a picaresque figure of whom Sir Walter Scott, one of his contemporaries, wrote in his novel *Waverley* 'he seemed to have lived a century too late, whose will was law to his sept'. From the moment of his chiefship he decided to live in the splendid traditional manner of his ancestors. Wherever he went, therefore, he was accompanied by his celebrated 'Glengarry Tail', a retinue of retainers all in full Highland dress who also guarded the castle entrance. They were swarthy, powerful, raw-boned retainers, each with his own ghillie to carry the swords, shields, and huge long-barrelled guns which went everywhere on the march. The Colonel himself proudly wore in his bonnet the eagle feather only worn by a chief. He kept his own private blind bard, Ailean Dall, in full ceremonial costume, who delivered true bardic orations at his arrival and departure. He had also a private seer, or crystal gazer. In spite of all his eccentricities he was a man of great spirit, high personal courage, and acute common sense, though utterly indifferent of expenses incurred by his extravagant household.

When George IV visited Edinburgh in 1822 Glengarry claimed to be, with his 'tail', part of the royal bodyguard as sole representative of the Highland chiefs, a request graciously granted by the sovereign, who was both alarmed and amused at the full ceremonial splendour of the chief and his 'tail'.

Some time later, at a ball held in Inverness, Glengarry's request to a lady to dance with him was refused. It was not until he saw the same lady dancing with a young subaltern called Norman McLeod, grandson of the famous Flora Macdonald who helped Bonnie Prince Charlie to escape to Skye, that his fury and jealousy broke. He went straight up to the subaltern and publicly first insulted and then caned him. A challenge was promptly issued and accepted, and although Glengarry made an apology the subaltern would only agree to have honour satisfied if Glengarry allowed himself to be caned publicly in return. This was refused, and in the subsequent pistol duel Glengarry killed his opponent. Though charged with murder at Inverness he was unaccountably acquitted.

Glengarry was himself killed shortly after when attempting and failing to get ashore from a wrecked steamer. His funeral was bizarre indeed, and certainly the last of its kind to be seen in Scotland. When his clansmen heard a hearse was to be sent to the castle they threatened to smash it to pieces the moment it entered the glen 'for it is by the hands of the people, and shoulder high, that their chief should be borne to his grave. Never shall we see him carried in a cart'. And so at dawn, headed by their own piper, they came on to the castle lawn and at the entrance to the castle hung the Gaelic yellow clan banner, and into the decorative antlers of the stags set upon the castle walls inserted lighted wax tapers.

Four clansmen, including the head of the cadet line, then took up the coffin. Four others bearing lighted torches stood at each corner, moving solemnly off as the piper began to play 'The Chief's Lament'. It was a bitter January day, and a sudden thunderstorm with cold drenching rain was thought a bad omen indeed to the mourners behind the solemn cortège. As the procession entered the glen the blind bard began his dirge, waving his bonnet and crying aloud 'Ochan. Ochan. Ochan.'

As they drew near the little stream dividing them from the cemetery they found it a swollen raging torrent instead of a trickle of water, and precariously balancing the coffin were obliged to plunge into the icy water. As they did so the eldest son of the dead chief cried with loud defiance from the other side the ancient Glengarry battle cry.

After the funeral, when the will was proved, there were debts of £80,000, an immense sum in those days, and all the estates had to be sold to pay for the years of ceremonial splendour and glory enjoyed by its late chief.

Before this event a mass emigration from the Highlands in general and Glengarry in particular had begun. The introduction of the potato by one of the Macdonalds, and later the black-faced sheep, caused immense poverty, and led by their priest hundreds of Glengarry tenants emigrated to Canada, depopulating the glens. There they founded their first settlement in 1786, in Upper Canada, calling it Glengarry. Here, also, they raised the famous regiment known as the Glengarry Fencibles, later the Glengarry Highlanders, who played so great a part in 1812–14 when America attempted to conquer Canada. All their former renowned ferocity in war won them both respect and fear, and so their great Highland traditions lived on in a land far away indeed from the western isles of Scotland, of which they were once the proud and unchallenged lords.

MACLEAN OF DUART

Arms: Quarterly; 1, argent, a rock gules; 2, argent, a dexter hand fesswise couped gules holding a cross-crosslet fitchee in pale azure; 3, or, a lymphad oars in saltire and sails furled sable flagged gules; 4, argent, a salmon naiant ppr; in chief two eagles heads respectant gules.

The thirteenth-century Duart Castle, home of the clan Maclean of Duart, stands on the extreme north-east part of the Scottish Isle of Mull, a jet-black perpendicular rock originally known as 'Black Height', rising almost 100 feet from the sea and visible for miles.

It is as formidable by land as by sea, and its present fine state of preservation after 700 years is due entirely to two of its great chiefs, Sir Lachlan Mor, who greatly enlarged and strengthened it in the seventeenth century, and Sir Fitzroy who, in the nineteenth century, rebuilt it from its former almost total ruin.

When as a boy of fifteen Sir Fitzroy had first seen the ancient family home and stronghold in a sprawling mass of ruins, he had sworn a solemn oath he would one day restore it to its former glory. This he finally did, though it took him sixty years.

The clansmen came to his summons from all over the world (as they still do), from America, Canada, New Zealand, Australia, Germany, Holland and other European countries. On the appointed day they assembled outside the castle walls to hear a messenger cry out: 'Is it your wish the chief know of your desire to see him?' A great roar of assent went up, then Maclean of Ardgour beat upon the castle door with his staff. It was opened by the grand old chief himself, now seventy-five. As the pipers played 'The Chief's Lament' the Maclean banner unfurled and proudly flew from the castle ramparts for the first time in 200 years.

In the courtyard stands a rowan tree, planted by the chief on his hundredth birthday, as a symbol to ward off evil spirits and thereby preserve safe keeping and well-being.

If any evidence were lacking of overseas contribution to the clan, visitors have only to see within the castle the silk regimental colours of the famous Maclean Kilties of America, the stars and stripes of the New York Scottish of New York, the French tricolour presented by Boston, Massachusetts, and the Union flag presented by New York.

The Macleans took their origin from the early tenth century Gillian Na Tuaighe 'the axe-bearing servant of John'. The first recorded chief, however, was Lachlan Lubernach, who in 1366 was given lands in Mull by Macdonald, Lord of the Isles, as well as his daughter in marriage. He probably built the massive keep of Duart Castle at about the same time. Both he and his son Eachunn Ruadh, or 'Hector of the Battleaxe' served their Macdonald overlords loyally. Hector was one of the finest swordsmen of his time, so renowned for his prowess that knights competed to combat with him. One of them, a Norwegian, fought to the death with Hector at Salen, Isle of Mull, and a green mound and cairn on the seashore covers the body of the slain Norwegian.

Hector himself, wielding his massive broadsword, fell in the bloody battle of Harlaw, both he and his enemy actually fighting foot to foot. Hector's body was carried from the field on the shields of the Innes and Ilvurrich clans and buried in Iona.

His great-great-grandson, Lachlan Cattanach, was probably the most ferocious of all the Duart chieftains. Not far from Duart Castle and out to sea, is the famous 'Lady's Rock', to which he had his wife rowed, put ashore, and left to drown at high tide. She was a daughter of the second Earl of Argyll, and both bride and bridegroom soon developed an uneasy and mutual dislike of each other.

Lachlan suspected her father of using her to secure her husband's lands, and his wife of secretly planning to poison him. She, curiously enough, took strong exception to his habit of taking his huge, unsheathed, razor-sharp broadsword to bed with him, which was scarcely conducive to marital pleasure.

She was fortunately rescued by some of her kinsmen passing in a boat, and was hidden away from her husband while he acted out his grief at a mock funeral of her supposed body, and Lachlan was promptly murdered by his brother-in-law as a revenge.

His second son, Allein Nan Sop, or 'Allan o' the Wisp' because he set fire to the straw-roofed buildings of his victims, was notorious in legend. As under feudal clan law he could not inherit from his father he took to piracy, first murdering his kinsman Maclean of Torloisk and taking all his lands. From Jura and Tarbat he plundered Bute, Lennox, Renfrew, and even Ireland. He managed to die peacefully in bed when he was quite old, unmarried, but with two bastard sons. Over his tomb in Iona is a carving of the galley he used for his piratical raids.

His great-nephew, Lachlan Mor, a man of herculean strength and courage, became head of the house of Duart, his chiefship beginning and ending in disaster. His secret and very profitable pact with Queen Elizabeth to prevent Catholic mercenaries from Spain reaching Ireland via the Western Isles to continue the Irish wars, was foiled by a savage and bloody war which suddenly broke out between the Macleans and their overlords the Macdonalds at about the time the *Florencion*, one of the Spanish Armada galleons, was forced into Tobermory Bay by a storm.

It carried a crew of 300, fifty-six guns, and an estimated £30,000,000, as well as a lady of high rank and a Spanish grandee as captain. His arrogant demand to Maclean to provision his ship was angrily refused, but after hard bargaining provisions were exchanged for 100 Spanish marines to help the Macleans slaughter the Macdonalds, which they at once proceeded to do.

When the Spaniard, anxious to sail, demanded the return of his men Maclean held three of the officers as hostages, whilst sending the rest and Donald Maclean, only son of Maclean of Morvern, to complete the bargain. Donald, however, was immediately disarmed and imprisoned below deck, but during the night he succeeded in laying a train to the powder magazine next to his cabin and at dawn the next day blew the ship to pieces, most of it sinking. It is a treasure ship which never ceases to attract divers ready to retrieve its vast wealth. Concession to do so was granted by Charles I to the dukes of Argyll.

Lachlan himself was later killed in a bloody battle, after commanding his badly wounded son to flee and revenge him. His body was carried from the field by two mourning women who placed it in a cart and buried it in a churchyard nearby.

When James I came to the English throne he decided to subdue the enormous power of the various clan chieftains, and at once ordered Lachlan's son, Hector Og, to surrender Duart Castle for payment of rents due to the Crown. Though the castle was restored to him the following year a grave precedent had thus been established. Later on Hector was arrested for debt and this time Duart Castle was given to Sir Rory Mackenzie. From that time James viciously ordered the Marquess of Huntly to 'wipe out' the Macleans, but he had seriously underestimated the power and courage of this clan. It is all the more astonishing, therefore, that from that time onwards they became dedicated partisans of the house of Stuart.

Hector Og had two sons, Hector Mor and Sir Lachlan, both of whom in turn succeeded him. The latter, a man of elegance and foresight helped to make Duart Castle what it is today, leaving his initials *SML* and the date 1633 on the lintel above the main castle door for all his clan to see. James I, who always needed money, sold peerages and honours with total indiscrimination, and created him a Baron of Nova Scotia for a suitable sum, and for a little more a Baron of Morvern, but he was ordered to hand back Iona.

The wily Duke of Argyll, by offering to buy Maclean's debts to the crown, lent him the necessary money, and thus began the blackmail which almost brought the house of Maclean to total ruin with each fresh twist of the Argyll screw. When, later, Maclean fully realised his position and came to remonstrate with Argyll he found himself flung into prison at Carrick Castle and not released until he gave his bond to pay Argyll £30,000 in Scots money. On his release Sir Lachlan at once dispossessed himself of all his lands to his son and successor, keeping only a life interest. After his death he was buried in Iona.

When his son Hector Ruadh succeeded him the Argyll debt had more than doubled. The wars of Montrose, whom the Macleans supported and the Argylls opposed, added enormously to the cost as they pitilessly plundered, looted, and burned each other's lands. This did not prevent Hector Ruadh from continuing to support the Stuart cause.

He was succeeded by his brother Sir Allan, a ten-year-old boy in ward to his uncle Donald of Brolas, under whose guidance he tried to settle the Argyll debt, now over £121,000—more than four times the original sum. But the Argyll Synod was pitiless and foreclosed, thus securing Duart Castle, Morvern, and Tiree until the debt was fully recovered by collected rents.

Another minor, John, only four years old, became head of the Duart line under two kinsmen tutors. His whole life was a nightmare of debt, persecution, even treason and rebellion, or so the Argylls alleged, and the bitter feud between the clans now broke into open warfare. Argyll fell upon all the remaining estates, lands, and castles of Maclean until all that was left to John was a now astronomical debt of £200,000 in Scots money, his title, and a pension of £300 granted to him by the Privy Council.

Then the Argylls themselves became forfeit and the Duart lands came back once more into the hands of Sir John's tutors. They, however, dying within a year of each other, left the chief to make what he could of his plundered land, though this was to be short-lived.

Sir John, now in France with James VII, who had received him well, returned with him to England to regain possession of the English throne held by William of Orange, a venture which ended in the total defeat of the Stuarts at the Boyne, leaving William and Mary on the throne. Argyll was again restored because of his Protestant allegiance and thus once more in possession of the Maclean lands. Sir John was not only compelled to surrender his castles and the family home of Duart, but as extra salt in the wound, forced to take an oath of allegiance to William. After James was defeated Sir John fled to France as an exile, and was only allowed to return to England by Queen Anne as a reward for his loyalty to the Stuart cause.

Yet once more, in the Rising of 1715, Sir John, under the Earl of Mar, made another ill-fated and desperate attempt to restore the Stuarts. Imprisoned at Fort William, he made his escape, caught a severe chill and died of consumption, a greatly loved and esteemed chief, some said the greatest of all the chiefs.

Sir Hector, his son who succeeded him, was born in Calais and, as a student in Edinburgh, was already planning to head the landing in Scotland of Bonnie Prince Charlie. He was betrayed by one named Blair, arrested, imprisoned in Edinburgh Castle where he was examined for several hours and then sent on to London and the Tower for further questioning.

As the King of France guaranteed him unlimited credit and a safe conduct he was returned to that country. From Paris he went on to Rome where he had an apoplectic fit, recovered, had a second attack and died, the last of his line since he was succeeded by Allan, fourth chief of the Macleans of Brolas.

During his imprisonment the bloody battle of Culloden had been fought, and not having their own chief the clan fought under Maclean of Drimnin. It was the end of the powerful hereditary feudal clan system as far as this could be achieved militarily. In spite of it, however, neither the Hanoverians, nor indeed any successive government, has ever been able to destroy the devotion, love, loyalty and pride the clansmen had for their chief, for whom they were at all times prepared to fight and die.

Altera merces or 'Reward is secondary' was one of their ancient battle cries. Rewards have indeed come grudgingly, if at all, from those very sovereigns they so loyally supported throughout the 700 years of their eventful and stormy history.

It was finally that grand old man Sir Fitzroy Donald Maclean, tenth baronet and twenty-sixth chief of the clan who restored Duart Castle as the proud family home it is today, to which so many thousands of visitors have gone and been so courteously received.

The present great chief is Baron Maclean of Duart and Morvern in the county of Argyll. He is a Knight of the Thistle, Lord Chamberlain, and until recently dedicated Chief Scout of the British Commonwealth.

MACKENZIE

Earls of Seaforth

Arms: Azure, a stag's head caboshed or.

The royal and ancient Scottish castle of Eilean Donan, near Dornie in Wester Ross, is almost the perfect romantic castle, set as it is amongst some of the finest scenery in Scotland. It was once the home of the great clan of Mackenzie, who later became the earls of Seaforth, doomed to extinction by a terrible curse put upon them. By courtesy of the MacRae family whose ancestors were constables of the castle under the earls of Seaforth, countless people are able to visit it annually.

This once impregnable stronghold, built originally against the invasions of the Norsemen and the Danes, stands on a rocky promontory where the three sea lochs of Long, Duich, and Aish meet, and looks towards the dense tree-covered hills of the opposite shore reflected in the still, deep waters as if in a mirror.

The origin of the Mackenzies, like so many other ancient and historic Highland families, is speculative and conflicting. It is generally accepted, however, and certainly by its own clan historian, that they descended from Gillion Og, or Colin the Younger, whose father, Colin of the Aird, was the ancestor of the powerful earls of Ross, overlords of the Mackenzies until the forfeiture of the Lordship of the Isles in 1493.

Another authority, however, states that they originated with Colin FitzGerald, a cadet of the ancient Irish house of Geraldine, who, having been driven out of his own country sought refuge in Scotland. As a reward for his valour at the battle of Largs he received from Alexander III, in 1266, the first free feudal barony of Kintail. He was also appointed Governor of the royal castle of Eilean Donan, and married the daughter of the Lord High Steward of Scotland.

It is said that his son Kenneth, who succeeded as second baron, later saved this king's life from a stag at bay whilst out hunting, cutting off its head with one blow of his sword, whence he was known as Caberface or stag's head, and at once took it as the well-known Mackenzie coat of arms.

Kenneth became not only a powerful but a popular chief, largely because of his triumphant defeat of the detested clan overlord, the third Earl of Ross, who in an attempt to storm and capture the castle of Eilean Donan was driven back with great slaughter.

Kenneth also built the famous Brahan Castle on the road from Beauly to the Muir of Ord in Ross and Cromarty, one of the three most northerly Scottish counties. This became the family home of the Mackenzies and was regarded almost with reverence by the clan. He it was who became the ancestor of the house of Seaforth, and it was in this castle that the terrible curse on the family was first uttered which ended with the death of the last earl some 150 years later, and all his sons.

He was succeeded by his son John, who sheltered Robert the Bruce after his defeat by Macdougall of Lorne in the War of Independence, and was later rewarded for his services by liberal grants of land from the forfeited Ross clan, thus becoming one of the most powerful Highland chieftains. By the beginning of the seventeenth century the Mackenzies possessed all the Highlands and the coveted Western Isles, either in their own right or through overlordship.

By a curious coincidence each of the first six feudal chiefs of Kintail had only one lawful son to succeed, and each in turn continued the ceaseless and bloody feuds with rival clans, as well as fighting with great distinction in the battles of Bannockburn, Flodden, Pinkie, and Otterburn.

Colin 'the One Eyed', eleventh chief, fought on the side of Queen Mary in the battle of Langside, which finally ruined her interests in Scotland and nearly cost him his life. He was fortunate enough to earn a remission for his actions and was even later made a privy councillor by James VI.

Kenneth, his son by Barbara Grant of that ilk, was raised to the peerage as Lord Mackenzie of Kintail. His brother, Sir Roderick of Tarbat, was the ancestor of the Cromarty line, his son John being created a Baronet of Nova Scotia and his grandson, Sir George Mackenzie, a man of very great learning, was created the first Earl of Cromarty, Viscount of Tarbat, and Lord Macleod and Castlehaven, titles borne by the extant house of Cromarty.

Colin, successor to Kenneth, was elevated to the peerage in 1633 by James VI as the first Earl of Seaforth, but as both he and his brother died unmarried the title devolved upon their half-brother George, a fickle, unstable character. He began by supporting Charles I in Scotland, in command of a large force of Covenanters, but finding little heart in his cause was imprisoned as a Royalist. On his release he went over to Montrose, who had himself seceded from the Covenanters.

The earl, at the head of 5,000 men, was defeated and sentenced by the General Assembly as 'an excommunicated traitor', and threatened with forfeiture of all his honours and titles. He was instead imprisoned for two years and only with great difficulty had himself released from the dreaded sentence of excommunication. After the execution of Charles I he fled into exile, dying in Holland in 1651.

His son, Kenneth, third earl, was a fervent Royalist, and having been taken prisoner at the battle of Worcester was totally excepted from Cromwell's Act of Grace and Pardon. All his estates were forfeited and no provision at all allowed to his wife and children.

After the Restoration the earl went to Paris and as his absence became more and more prolonged, the by now suspicious, angry and embittered Countess decided to resort to the power of magic. Before her marriage Isabella had been the daughter of John Mackenzie of Tarbat, thus descended from the earl's own family, and was sister of the first Earl of Cromartie. It was this cruel, vindictive woman who finally brought down the house of Seaforth.

Not far away, at Strathpeffer, lived 'The Warlock of the Glen', a celebrated crystal gazer renowned all over Scotland for his extraordinary gift of second sight. She sent a messenger to summon him to the castle where, after some long time looking through his crystal, which was a curious white stone with a hole in the middle, the seer told her that the earl was not only safe but well and merry.

The countess, whose suspicions were now even stronger, demanded further details, persisting in her demands, cajoling, entreating, and finally threatening him with unspeakable punishment if he did not tell her all that he knew and had seen. At last he answered, 'Since you force me to tell you what will only make you unhappy I will do so'. He then told her he had seen her husband in a large and sumptuously furnished room in Paris. On his lap was a most beautiful woman whose hand was pressed to his lips whilst his arms were round her waist.

In a furious burst of uncontrollable anger the countess viciously called him a liar, a traducer, a defamer of her lord in his own castle and before his own vassals. Scorned by her husband, humiliated before her servants, and beyond all reason now, she ordered a gallows to be erected and the seer to be hanged as soon as possible. She refused absolutely all appeals for mercy and left him to the fate she had decreed.

Just before his death the seer gazed once more into his crystal before throwing it into the loch and uttered the terrible curse which the Highlanders talk of to this very day.

I see into the far future and I read the doom of the race of Seaforth which will end in sorrow and extinction. I see a chief, the last of his house, both deaf and dumb, the father of four sons all of whom he will follow to the grave, and no future chief of the Mackenzie clan shall reside at Brahan or in Kintail. All his possessions shall be inherited by a white-hooded lassie from the East who shall kill her own sister. As a sign all these things shall come to pass there shall be four great lairds in the last days of the deaf and dumb Seaforth. One shall be buck-toothed, one hare-lipped, one half-witted, and one a stammerer.

Every single detail of this prophecy was to come true, though almost 150 years were to pass before its fulfilment.

Kenneth, the fourth earl, was also a fanatical Royalist, suffering greatly for his loyalty by repeated imprisonment, finally dying in exile. King James had created him Marquess of Seaforth, a title only recognised by the Jacobites and not acknowledged by the British government. He had made a distinguished marriage with a daughter of William Herbert, Marquess of Powys.

William, the son of this marriage, was naturally a great Jacobite, coming to England when the Earl of Mar raised his standard at Braemar, but after being defeated at the head of some 3,000 men he fled back to France, having had all his titles and estates forfeited. In 1719, however, and undeterred by his very considerable losses, he made one last effort 'to bring the auld Stewarts back again'.

This time he was dangerously wounded on his own estates at Glen Shiel. The Mackenzies and the two devoted septs, the MacRaes and the Maclennans, carried their wounded chief away in the night to where a secret vessel was waiting off the coast which took him by way of the Western Isles back to France.

Though his estates had all been forfeited, all efforts by the government to collect the rents failed, their soldiers being driven out and even killed by the wild MacRaes, so that the whole dangerous scheme was abandoned. Instead, the clansmen themselves collected the rents, and for ten years Donald Murchison, son of the castellan of Eilean Donan Castle and the earl's factor, went to and fro between Scotland and France with the money.

The earl was finally pardoned for life by George I. He died in 1740 and would have been succeeded as sixth earl by his son Kenneth, who was given the courtesy title in the Irish peerage of Lord Fortrose, but for the attainder. His grandson, however, re-purchased all the estates from the Crown, was raised to Viscount Fortrose in the Irish peerage and had restored to him the earldom of Seaforth.

As he died unmarried he was succeeded by his brother Francis Humberston Mackenzie, twenty-first chief of the clan, who was created a peer in Great Britain as Lord Seaforth and Baron Mackenzie of Kintail. It was on him, the last Earl of Seaforth that the terrible curse finally fell.

At the age of twelve, owing to scarlet fever, the earl became stone deaf and for a time dumb, though the latter handicap he mastered and regained his speech. He was a great lover of art, natural history, and military science. He personally raised a splendid regiment which became the famous Seaforth Highlanders, and was later Governor of Barbadoes, all remarkable achievements for a man with his handicap. He had by his marriage four sons and six daughters.

The prophesied four lairds appeared, one buck-toothed, one hare-lipped, one half-witted, and the fourth a stammerer. First one of his sons died, then a second and a third, the fourth becoming critically ill in the south of England. When news of his death reached the earl at Brahan Castle he became not only dumb but almost insane before he too died, the house of Seaforth becoming extinct in the male line.

To complete the curse, his eldest daughter, knowing nothing of it, returned to Scotland from India after the death of her husband, Admiral Sir Samuel Hood. She wore the white hood of a widow. Later, whilst driving a pony and trap, she had an accident which resulted in the death of her sister. Thus every single detail of the terrible Brahan Castle curse was relentlessly carried out, becoming a legend in any history of the Scottish Highland clans.

All that remains today of the ancient and illustrious house of Seaforth are the two ruined castles of Brahan and Eilean Donan, the forest of Kintail, and the famous Highland regiment proudly bearing its name, now the Queen's Own Highlanders.

BIBLIOGRAPHY

Beyond the main and indispensable sources of the *Visitations of the Heralds*, the *Victoria County Histories*, *Dictionary of National Biography*, G. C. Cockayne's *Complete Peerage*, W. Berry's *County Genealogies*, Sir Bernard Burke's *Vicissitudes of Families*, and the various works on extinct and extant peerages, baronetages, knightages, and landed gentry of T. C. Banks, J. and J. B. Burke, A. Collins, Sir William Dugdale, and Foster, the following authorities have been widely used.

Aubrey, J. *Brief Lives*, Oxford 1898, reprint London 1949
Barton, S. *Castles in Britain*, Worthing 1973
Bindoff, S. T. *Tudor England*, Harmondsworth 1950
Boutell, C. *Heraldry*, 1867, reprint London 1950
Bulwer Lytton, E. *The Last of the Barons*, London 1843, reprint London 1906
Burrows, M. *The Family of Brocas . . .*, London 1886
Dunbar, J. G. *The Historic Architecture of Scotland*, London 1906
Dunlop, J. *The Clan Mackenzie*, Edinburgh 1952
Froissart, J. *Chronicles*, Paris 1505, reprint Harmondsworth 1967
Grant, L. F. *The Clan Donald*, Edinburgh 1952
Halliday, F. E. *A History of Cornwall*, London 1959
Macaulay, T. B. *Critical & Historical Essays*, London 1843
Mackechnie, J. *The Clan Maclean*, Edinburgh 1952
McKerral, A. *The Clan Campbell*, Edinburgh 1953
Marshall, G. W. *The Genealogist's Guide*, London 1879, reprint London 1967
Miller, A. C. *Sir Henry Killigrew*, Leicester 1963
Peter, T. *History of Cornwall*, Truro 1906
Pevsner, N. *The Buildings of England*, Harmondsworth 1951 et seq
Planche, J. R. *The Pursuivant of Arms*, London 1851
Rowse, A. L. *Tudor Cornwall*, London 1941

Roddis, R. J. *The History of Penryn*, Truro 1964

Scott-Giles, C. W. *Shakespeare's Heraldry*, London 1950

Simpson, W. D. *Castles in England & Wales*, London 1969

Smyth, J. *Lives of the Berkeleys*, London 1821, reprint London 1883

Sorrell, A. *Living history*, London 1969

Stuart and Paul. *Scottish family history*, Edinburgh 1936

Taylor, J. *Great Historic Families of Scotland*, London 1887

Toy, S. *The Castles of Great Britain*, London 1953

Tranter, N. G. *The Fortified House in Scotland*, Edinburgh 1962

Trevelyan, G. M. *History of England*, London 1926, reprint Harmondsworth 1959

Tytler, P. F. *History of Scotland*, Edinburgh 1867

Wagner, A. *English Ancestry*, London 1961

Wedgwood, C. V. *The King's Peace*, London 1955
The Trial of Charles I, London 1964

William of Malmesbury. *Chronicles of the kings of England*, London 1847

Woodward, J. *Treatise of Heraldry*, London & Edinburgh 1892, reprint Newton Abbot 1969

ACKNOWLEDGEMENTS

I should like to express my thanks to the many reference libraries who have been so helpful to me; to Mrs M. Joyce, Miss E. R. Pool, Mrs D. Miller, and Mr Gus Edwards for their individual assistance.

I owe a deep debt of gratitude to my brother Geoffrey for his painstaking, meticulous, and often illuminating research, as well as his patience and understanding kindness throughout.

I wish also to thank Keith B. Steadman, not only for his splendid illustrations but for the peace and quiet of his house and beautiful garden where most of this book has been written.

Last and most of all, my inexpressible gratitude to Madeline Paul for the countless hours she has spent taping, typing, checking and revising my manuscript, for without her wholly invaluable co-operation throughout the two years it has taken to write this book it could never have been achieved.

Keith B. Poole.